THE MILLENNIUM TIME BOMB

A PRACTICAL GUIDE TO THE TECHNICAL AND LEGAL ISSUES

CAROLINE BRAMLEY,
Cambridgeshire County Council
AND
SIMON HALBERSTAM,
Halberstam Elias

INSTITUTE OF DIRECTORS

KOGAN PAGE

YOURS TO HAVE AND TO HOLD
BUT NOT TO COPY

First published in 1998

Apart from any fair dealing for the purposes of research or private study, or criticism or review, as permitted under the Copyright, Designs and Patents Act 1988, this publication may only be reproduced, stored or transmitted, in any form or by any means, with the prior permission in writing of the publishers, or in the case of reprographic reproduction, in accordance with the terms and licences issued by the CLA. Enquiries concerning reproduction outside those terms should be sent to the publishers at the undermentioned address:

Kogan Page Limited
120 Pentonville Road
London N1 9JN
UK

Kogan Page Limited
163 Central Avenue, Suite 4
Dover
NH 03820
USA

KINGSTON UPON HULL CITY LIBRARIES	
B386356369	
Morley Books	29.10.98
005.16 RT	£16.99
	HCT

The Institute of Directors accepts no responsibility for the opinions expressed by the authors of this publication. Readers should consult their advisors before acting on any of the issues raised.

© Simon Halberstam and Cambridgeshire County Council 1998

The right of Simon Halberstam and Caroline Bramley to be identified as the authors of this work has been asserted by them in accordance with the Copyright, Designs and Patents Act 1988.

British Library Cataloguing in Publication Data

A CIP record for this book is available from the British Library.

ISBN 0 7494 2707 8

Typeset by Saxon Graphics Ltd, Derby
Printed and bound in Great Britain by
Biddles Ltd, Guildford and King's Lynn

Contents

ABOUT THE AUTHORS	vi
INTRODUCTION	xi

PART ONE – THE TECHNICAL ISSUES

CHAPTER 1
The Problem – What is this Millennium Bug fuss all about?   3

CHAPTER 2
The Implications – OK, so there's a big computer problem – why should I be concerned?   9

CHAPTER 3
Project Management – OK, I understand the problem and how it could affect my business, but what on earth can I do about it?   15

CHAPTER 4
Inventory – Make a detailed list of all those parts of your operation that could be affected!   23

CHAPTER 5
Planning – Make a plan to deal with the problems you face!   33

CHAPTER 6
Prioritize/Investigate/Decide – Right – I've got my inventory and plan, but what do I do now?   41

CHAPTER 7
More Planning – Be prepared for shocks – and plan how to cope with them!   61

CHAPTER 8
The Ongoing Project – Get on with it!   71

PART TWO – THE LEGAL ISSUES

CHAPTER 9
Contract Law – Defining Relationships – Which of your business relationships are going to be affected by the Millennium Bug?   75

CHAPTER 10
Contract Law – Relevant Principles and Issues – How to determine what contractual rights you may have against your suppliers   105

CHAPTER 11
Contract Law – Remedies for Breach of Contract – Recovering damages and other forms of relief against the suppliers who cause your problems   131

CHAPTER 12
Tort – If others have caused us loss through their negligent actions or statements, what are our legal rights?   141

CHAPTER 13
The Position and Duties of Directors – Personal liability of directors who fail to safeguard the interests of the company   155

CHAPTER 14
The Annual Audit – What will your auditors do if they find that the Year 2000 might threaten your commercial survival?   163

CHAPTER 15
Due Diligence – Mergers and Acquisitions – Should you take the Year 2000 risk?   169

CHAPTER 16
Data Protection – Could the Year 2000 cause you to infringe the laws relating to personal data?   175

CHAPTER 17
Litigation and Other Forms of Dispute Resolution – How
to recover your losses and enforce your remedies   179

APPENDIX A
**BSI Year 2000 Compliance Definition and Associated
Documentation**   191

APPENDIX B
Model Year 2000 Software Compliance Questionnaire   195

Appendix C
**Model Request for Year 2000 Compliance Statement and
Warranty to be Sent to Suppliers**   201

APPENDIX D
Model Year 2000 Compliance Warranty   205

INDEX   **207**

About the authors

Caroline Bramley was born in Birmingham and studied Classics at Cambridge University. After a brief career as a teacher she joined Cambridgeshire County Council as a trainee programmer and has worked there ever since – over 20 years.

After having been Operational Support Manager for many years she now works as Corporate IT Client Manager, managing the budget for corporate systems such as electronic mail, personnel and intranet systems, as well as being responsible for developing IT training facilities and liaison across the County's IT community.

In 1995 she was incautious enough to raise the Millennium Bug issue at the Council – and was promptly given the job of co-ordinating the County's many Millennium projects.

After obtaining both French Law and English Law degrees, **Simon Halberstam** became a specialist in Information Technology Law. He is head of IT Law and the Year 2000 Law Group at Halberstam Elias & Co. Halberstam Elias is a leading IT/Internet law firm based in London and is now also recognized as one of the top firms in the Year 2000 arena.

The firm advised the British Standards Institute in its Year 2000 Conformity Requirements definition as reproduced in Appendix 4. This definition has now become the *de facto* national standard.

The Halberstam Elias website at www.weblaw.co.uk hosts the database of Year 2000-compliant products, which have been endorsed by the Computer Software and Services Association, the IBM Computer Users' Association and other major bodies. Halberstam Elias runs a free Year 2000 legal hotline, which can be accessed on 0171 405 5382 or via e-mail to law@weblaw.co.uk

Foreword

When I first became involved in the Year 2000 challenge, I thought I had a good idea of what the future had in store for us. Oh boy, have I been surprised!

Since 1995 I've travelled over half a million miles around the globe talking to business leaders, government departments and the media about the Year 2000 problem. I've addressed 300 conferences on the subject and the pace seems set to increase as we approach the end of the century. Audiences always produce an endless stream of technical questions but it is when the legal implications are discussed that most confusion arises.

If, like many of the people I address, you're concerned about your rights and responsibilities surrounding this issue, you're holding a golden key in your hands. This book answers the questions that are continuously put to me by business leaders everywhere in the world. While there are plenty of books covering the technical aspects of the Year 2000 challenge, Caroline Bramley and Simon Halberstam have put together the most comprehensive practical guide I have found anywhere in the world on what this problem means to your business.

Caroline's hands-on experience in planning and implementing Year 2000 projects is clearly evident and makes a refreshing change from the onlooker's perspective to which we are usually exposed. If there's anything to learn from one who's been there – and Caroline offers much – my advice is that you grab it with both hands.

Halberstam Elias is widely acknowledged as the leading law firm in the Year 2000 field. Through the firm's work for the IBM Computer Users' Association, Simon was at the legal forefront of this issue way before most people realized it even existed. He was the only lawyer on the team that formulated the British Standards Institution's Definition of Year 2000 Conformity Requirements, a definition that has been adopted as the national standard, not only in Britain but other countries too. His extensive knowledge is put across in a jargon-free style that stamps this as a book for smart business people, not for other lawyers. Simon has undertaken the arduous task of putting together the current collective wisdom on Year 2000 liability; negligence, personal responsibility; audits; due diligence; directors' duties to shareholders; and the changing data protection act – in short, everything you ever wanted to know about what the Year 2000 problem could mean to you.

The only issue not covered in this book is that of insurance. It's an issue clouded in unsettled dust at this stage. Rather than hypothesize, the authors have decided to focus on those issues where clear analysis and advice are possible. I believe this is the right decision – 2000 is one deadline that cannot be postponed and preparing for it is extraordinarily time-consuming. However, as Caroline demonstrates, the problem can be resolved.

The Year 2000 is rumbling – not always quietly – through the law courts, both in the UK and the USA. I don't think any of us will be at all surprised when the first class action suit – and there are six pending as I write this – is finally heard. Personally, I don't believe litigation is the way to go, nor do I believe that anyone will successfully take on America's mighty software corporations. There's no point. Even if you won, you'd still have a Year 2000 problem and your business would still be at risk. At every opportunity I put this key message across: the Year 2000 challenge is not about laying blame or waiting for someone else to fix it. It's about *you* taking ownership of *your* problems and making *your own* informed risk decisions.

As Simon makes crystal clear, you need to assess the risk to which your company is exposed. The only way to do this is to check not only every single PC and computer in your organization – and tools exist to help you do this automatically – but also the contracts governing the supply and maintenance of those systems as well as outsourcing arrangements. Then you can set about methodically dealing with the mission critical systems your diagnosis will have pinpointed, armed with the knowledge of whether you are legally entitled to look to suppliers and services providers to cover or contribute to remediation costs.

Don't be put off by anyone who says it's too late. It may be too late to fix everything but most of us would admit that we never use all of our computing hardware and software anyway. The good news is that it probably doesn't matter if you don't fix everything – as long as your mission critical systems survive. Start now along the path of year 2000 discovery and they will.

Good luck – and remember. 'The future ain't what it used to be'.

Karl W Feilder
President and CEO
Greenwich Mean Time

Acknowledgements

With thanks for their support and input to all the lawyers at Halberstam Elias & Co.

Simon Halberstam

I would like to thank all my colleagues for putting up with me while I wrote this book – but especially my thanks go to Ruth Revill for her assistance during the setting up of my own Millennium projects and for the Timeline plan – for it was her idea.

Caroline Bramley

The legal section of this book was written with the assistance of Gabrielle Halberstam, Jonathan Berman and other lawyers from the Year 2000, Internet, litigation and company/commercial departments at Halberstam Elias.

The permission of the British Standards Institute to include DISC PD 2000-1 'A Definition of Year 2000 Conformity Requirements' is hereby acknowledged.

Introduction

Readers will already have read and heard extensively about the disaster that awaits software users when the next Millennium dawns. Statistics about cost and impact of the Millennium change abound. One frequently asked question is how great the problem really is. Is it primarily scaremongering hyperbole or does it presage a global recession of catastrophic proportions?

The truthful answer is that nobody can gauge with any great degree of accuracy the global impact that the Year 2000 might bring in its wake. However, what is becoming increasingly clear is that unless many IT users address the issue very soon, many companies will suffer considerable disruption and losses when the new century arrives.

At the time of writing, it is estimated that about eighty per cent of 'blue chip' companies have a Year 2000 compliance project in place and that in the SME sector the equivalent figure is closer to twenty per cent. For the purposes of this book, when we use the terms 'Year 2000 compliant', 'compliance' and 'compliant' we refer to the British Standards Institution definition of 'Year 2000 Conformity' as reproduced in Appendix A.

The proliferation of compliance questionnaires in circulation bears witness to the relevance in this context of the words of John Donne – 'No man is an island'. Even those companies that manage to make their internal systems completely compliant are very likely to suffer problems as a result of the lack of compliance of their suppliers and customers. If your customers are not compliant, their resulting economic problems may impact on the level of business you derive from them or, even, their ability to survive. Moreover, if one of your key supplier's systems fails and it becomes unable to service your requirements, you in turn will probably become unable to meet your obligations to your customers.

The understandable tendency until the early months of 1998 has been to focus exclusively on the technical aspect of what is intrinsically a technical problem. However, as time elapses, awareness of the chain reaction phenomenon increases and, with funds running scarce in some cases, it becomes clear to many IT users that they cannot resolve all their potential Year 2000-related problems.

We are therefore witnessing what is known as 'triage', a process by which companies determine on which areas of their operation their compliance efforts should focus. The decisions as to which areas should be focused on at the sacrifice of others tends to fall to those unfortunate enough to have been appointed Year 2000 compliance project managers. These individuals are faced on a daily basis with invidious decisions which, should matters turn out badly, are likely to rebound on them rather painfully.

An important factor in their decision-making process is to determine those areas where they would have legal recourse should their companies suffer disruption and loss. In a nutshell, if we fail our customers because our suppliers fail us, can we recover our losses from them? This is essentially a legal issue dependent on the legal relationship between different entities and their respective rights and obligations. To determine this, a comprehensive audit of software, hardware and machinery contracts is necessary. Legal audits (as discussed in Chapter 9 below) are a key element in the risk management of the Year 2000 problem. They enable companies not only to identify their contractual strengths and weakness with a view to potential litigation but also may provide the lever necessary to avoid the need for litigation by bringing pressure on systems and services providers to sort out potential problems before their effects are felt. If one can demonstrate to suppliers that they would be contractually liable should a particular problem eventuate, they are far more likely to assist you in the prevention of that problem, whether their assistance be technical or financial.

Prevention in this context is obviously better than cure. This is particularly so as, even if one does not subscribe to the cataclysmic prophecies which abound, there is a good chance that potential targets may well have disappeared or gone 'bust' before one can sue them in the aftermath of the Year 2000.

The legal issues raised by the Year 2000 do not simply involve an analysis of corporate rights, obligations and liabilities. As directors have become aware that their personal liability may be engaged if they fail to implement proper Year 2000 programs, the jobs of Year 2000 project managers have become somewhat easier. The fact that auditors are threatening to qualify accounts of companies which have not budgeted and accounted properly for the costs and potential impact of the Year 2000 has also helped to focus the minds of directors. Thus, the book also considers the position of directors and the role of auditors.

The legal and technical facets of the Year 2000 may also have a braking effect on merger activity in the late 1990s as acquisitive companies start to wonder whether they may be buying their way into Year 2000-related problems. Not only might Year 2000 adversely affect the key IT systems and machinery of potential targets but also expose them to liability for the supply of non-compliant merchandise or the future inability to fulfil their contractual obligations. All of these factors will have to be examined in the context of due diligence, another legal topic which we consider in this book.

In previous works on the Year 2000, the focus has tended to be exclusively technical. However, as indicated above, while the essence of the problem is technical, the repercussions will be commercial and stem from the correlation between the technical and legal aspects. In this book, we have adopted a holistic approach and endeavoured to provide a comprehensive business guide to the Year 2000 by encompassing both the technical and legal ramifications.

Simon Halberstam
HALBERSTAM ELIAS & CO.

Caroline Bramley
CAMBRIDGESHIRE COUNTY COUNCIL

PART one
THE TECHNICAL ISSUES

The Problem

What is this Millennium Bug fuss all about?

For those of us programming 20 years or so ago, one of the most valuable and expensive of IT resources was space. Early computers had little storage or memory – so any technique that reduced the amount of data to be processed was to be applauded, and adopted. One of the easiest ways to compress data is to remove that which is either always going to be the same or can be very simply assumed. Dates were considered an easy target for compression, because the first part of the year, that is the two digits which denote the century, would be the same for the foreseeable future – they would always be '19'. Thus these were omitted when dates were stored, because the programmer could code statements to supply the missing digits where they were needed, ie for printing.

Dates, therefore, would be stored as follows:

13th May, 1953, would be stored as: 130553

or, more usually, as: 530513

as dates can be more easily manipulated in calculations if stored with the year first (see below).

This convenient and practical technique was soon adopted across the industry, and became the model for storing

THE TECHNICAL ISSUES

dates on most IBM compatible computers. As long as the programs only processed dates in the twentieth century, ie with years starting with '19', this would work perfectly. Obviously some programs, particularly those dealing with dates of birth, had to cope with years in the nineteenth century, but these were few, and the exception.

In the Year 2000, however, things will not be so convenient. Using such a technique the last day of the century, 31st December, 1999, is stored as: 991231

but 1st January, 2000, is: 000101.

The problem with this is clear. Computers on the whole cannot make assumptions – we would know, looking at the above dates, that the year in the second date is most probably 2000, but the computer has no way of knowing this. If the program is written on the basis that all the years start with '19', the computer will apply this to *every* date, however unlikely the result is, and will treat 000101 as 1st January, 1900. This simple misunderstanding is the basis of the Millennium problem.

So how will the problem manifest itself, and does it really matter if the computer thinks that it is 1900? A few simple examples will illustrate the effect. Take a program printing out cheques – usually it will process the cheque using today's date. The computer will think that it is 1st January, 1900 and the cheque will instantly be 100 years old; and even if the printed date could be ignored or interpreted, the computer will have recorded the date as 1900 and the cheque will be obsolete before it is drawn. Similarly a program registering births may well age new-born babies equally quickly, and staff may be retired before they have been born! Another problem is that the days of the week in 2000 are different from those in 1900. (1st January, 1900 was a Monday, 1st January, 2000 will be a Saturday.) Thus any program which deals with processes which trigger, say, every Monday, will get itself into a muddle once the century changes. In addition to this the Year 2000 is a leap year (this has been the subject of some debate, but it *is* a leap year), but 1900 was not (centuries need to be divisible by 400 rather than four to be leap years). The programs which assume that the year is 1900 will come to grief after 28th February.

Computers, however, use dates for a very wide range of processes, mainly based on the premise that dates stored with the year first get larger rather than smaller. The examples above illustrate problems which will be encountered by computers which need to store and/or print dates, or to process date-related activities. Where computers will also come badly to grief is where they need to manipulate the dates in calculations. Take for example a program which is calculating interest on a loan. Typically it needs to work out how long the loan has been held – so it will subtract one year from the other. Say the loan was taken out on 1st April, 1995. This will be stored as: 950401

and on 1st April, 1999 (stored as 990401) the program will do the following calculation:

990401 – 950401

and decide, correctly, that the loan is four years old. (This, incidentally, is the main reason why dates are stored year first, as this is necessary to process this sort of calculation easily.) On 1st April, 2000, however, the program will do this calculation:

000401 – 950401

and will come to the conclusion that the loan has been held for minus 95 years! (Most programs, however, do not expect to encounter negative lengths of time – so this program will either charge 95 years' interest, or, more likely, will fail completely! The program might, of course, charge –95 years' interest which would be fine if you have a loan, but not so good if you have a savings account!).

One thing that this example does illustrate is the unpredictable nature of the problem – without looking at the code it is impossible to know whether the program will charge the correct amount of interest, will charge 95 years'

THE TECHNICAL ISSUES

interest, will charge minus 95 years' interest, or fail completely! Any of these three possibilities could spell disaster for a loan company.

Another common process for computers is date validation. It is commonly, and correctly, held that if you put rubbish into computers you get rubbish out! For this reason computer programs tend to have complex validation processes built into them to ensure that any data stored is valid. Some of these validation processes will involve date validation – typically a program will check that the date in itself is valid (so, for instance, a computer which thinks that the year is 1900 will discard 29th February, even though this is valid for 2000), but also check that it is valid in conjunction with other dates. If we go back to the loan example above, the computer will check that the payment date is after the date of the start of the loan. A payment made on 1st April, 2000 (stored as 000401) will be compared against the date of the loan start (stored as 950401). A comparison of the two dates will tell the computer that the payment date (000401) is smaller than, ie before, the start of the loan (950401) and the date will fail the validation.

Using similar logic, the other main process used by computers which is date-related is sorting of dates. Frequently programs need to display records in date order, and these sort routines generally use the standard date storage format explained above. They also rely on the date getting 'larger' as the date gets later thus:

950401/960401/970401/980401/990401... etc.

In the Year 2000, however, this sort will fail. Because the year is '00' the sort will return:

000401/950401/960401... etc.

From the examples above it is easy to see the effect that the Millennium problem is going to have on even the simplest of computer programs. The problem is a very simple and straightforward one – so why the big panic? (and why, indeed, this book?) The answer to this lies not in the complexity of the problem but in its volume and its pervasiveness. The technique of storing dates was used not only in application programs, that is programs which perform the processes used in the examples above which are written to fulfil business requirements, but also in operating systems, that is those programs which control the computer's functions, and also in the chip at the very heart both of the computer and of most of the technology which we use today.

The Implications

OK, so there's a big computer problem – why should I be concerned?

Having established what the problem is and why it has been caused, you need to think carefully about the implications of this problem for your own organization. You are not helped in this by the amount of scare stories in the press. There is no doubt that some organizations will have bills in millions of pounds to deal with the Millennium – it is possible that there may be complete chaos and aeroplanes just might fall out of the sky! It is not easy, however, to equate these examples with your own organization, and it is, therefore, tricky for you to establish how you may be affected and, more importantly, to justify the expenditure to your directors – and this is crucial. Solving the problem is bound to cost you money and cause you disruption – you need to be able to convince your directors that the project is worthwhile *and* urgent! You will need to write a report or presentation to convince them, and the following tips may help you.

In order to establish the implications of the Millennium Bug you need to look at four areas of your organization:

THE TECHNICAL ISSUES

- computers and computer programs
- 'embedded chip' systems
- contracts
- suppliers and third parties.

You also need to consider two possible effects:
- failure
- inaccuracy (Don't forget this one – programs calculating inaccurately because they think the date is 1980 are almost more dangerous than programs which crash!).

You need to consider each of the two effects in relation to each of the four categories. If you are very aware of what IT you have, the first two categories will cause you no problems. Just go through your systems and pick out those which come instantly to mind and will make good, easily understood, examples. If you have no idea what IT you have, then you will have to wait until you have finished your inventory (see Chapter 4). For the purposes of your report you will need to pick business functions instead of IT systems and consider the implications of those failing instead.

Because of the amount of information available now you should not find it difficult to convince your directors of the importance of looking at software and computer hardware and even embedded chips. With the latter two categories, contracts and suppliers, you may have a more difficult job. You need to paint a picture of the possibility of your own organization spending huge sums to become compliant only to find that your important suppliers fail and you cannot continue in business. Similarly your main service or outsourcing contracts could fail and you need to bring this to the attention of your directors. Again choose examples which they will understand and will therefore have the effect you require – to frighten them into giving your project the go ahead!

Once you have chosen your examples you must also persuade them of the urgency and size of the problem. Remember:

- there are very few weeks now to the Millennium
- some programs will fail on 1st April, 1999, or even before that
- you may be unable to employ extra staff, or even to buy new PCs in 1999
- you may be unable to renew contracts for supplies and services in 1999

and

- you may have to replace all your PCs at £1000 each
- you may need to replace your servers – c£5–10,000 each
- you may have to replace your network
- you may have to employ consultants at £800+ per day
- you may have to replace your network and telephone system…
- etc, etc.

A good technique might be to draw attention to past computer projects and their timescale and costs. Try to make your point without panicking – use humour as well as scare tactics – and be as clear as you can! Figure 1 shows some examples of slides that may help your presentation.

YEAR TWO THOUSAND BECOMES 'A YEAR TO SHUTDOWN'

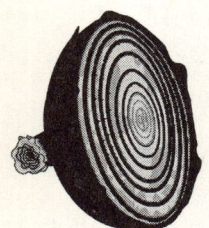

The Year 2000 is like an onion. As you peel the layers of problems from it, you find additional layers of problems waiting underneath, and, just like an onion, the more layers you peel from it the more you're going to cry.

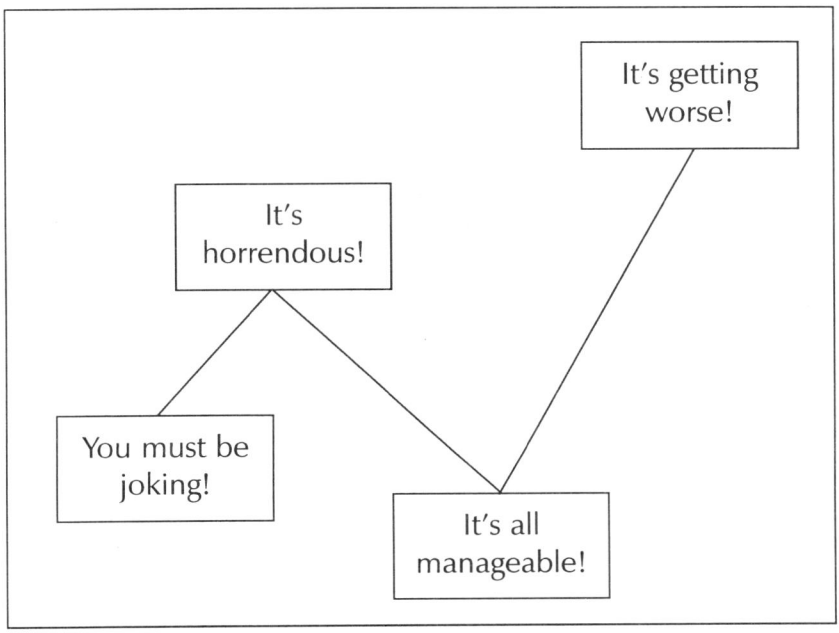

Figure 1 *Slides that may assist you in making a presentation to directors*

Project Management

OK, I understand the problem and how it could affect my business, but what on earth can I do about it?

Before you start this project you need to consider how you are going to manage it. You may be surprised to be reading this in a book about the Year 2000, and you may also consider that you already have experienced project managers and do not need any advice on the subject. But this project has two characteristics, which other projects you may have undertaken do not have:

- it is crucial for the survival of the organization
- it has a completely immovable end date.

Most projects, whether IT based or not, go over budget and over time. This project *cannot* go over time, and this must be managed differently from any other.

Whether you are a large or small organization, one of the most important actions to take before the project starts

THE TECHNICAL ISSUES

is to ensure that it is backed by the highest level of management that you can access. This project is so crucial to an organization that it must be seen to be backed by the most senior management. More important, perhaps, is the fact that the Year 2000 project is unlike any other. We have already dealt with some reasons why this is the case – the relevant issue here is that this project has many uncertainties. As investigations proceed, difficult decisions will need to be made about both money and priority, and the decisions will have to be made, or at least endorsed, by senior management.

Once you have senior management backing you need to decide how you wish to structure the project within your organization. This very much depends on the nature and size of your organization – it could be that you opt for one project team to cover all systems and departments, or alternatively you might decide that you need several different project teams running projects in several departments. Whatever structure you choose you need to have some sort of cross-organizational team whose role is particularly to ensure that the whole organization moves at the same pace. If you have one project team they could also fulfil this role – but if you have multi-departmental teams you need to ensure the following.

- There is a point into which each departmental team must report progress, and also, probably, cost estimates. Unless your organization is such that it can afford to allow one department to fail completely, this sort of liaison is crucial. In most organizations, even those with an extreme federal structure, there are some departmental functions which are critical to the organization as a whole. In such organizations the ultimate responsibility for the whole lies with the chief executive – he or she must be aware if a critical system is at risk and must be given the information to enable him or her to change

priorities if necessary. For instance in many public authorities the finance departments are frequently the biggest users of IT and the best organized in terms of Millennium projects. But, in fact, the highest priority system may well be the children at risk register. Real human and political damage could be done if this were not available. Thus, if there is any danger of this critical system failing, the chief executive must be informed so that he or she can shift corporate resources, both human and financial, from one project to another.
- There is a means of avoiding duplication. In some organizations there is corporate support for systems such as electronic mail, personnel, and a standard PC desktop. In other organizations this is left to departments. In all organizations, however, there is bound to be some duplication in use of hardware, software, and embedded chip technology. A cross-departmental liaison group can pool inventories and spot where there are duplicates. The necessary investigation work can then be shared between departments to save time and effort.
- A unified publicity/awareness initiative. Different organizations have different ways of communicating with their staff. But the Millennium problem is everybody's problem, not just an issue for IT staff. The organization's future depends on everybody. To make publicity and awareness effective it must work across the whole organization.
- An organization 'champion'. Even if departments run their own projects, it is useful to have an organizational 'champion' who can be a figurehead, a single point of contact, and a driver for the organization. But take care how you choose such a champion. Many people regard the Millennium as an IT 'trick' and will fail to be convinced by someone whom they regard as a newcomer or a smooth-talker – so don't choose a consultant as your champion! Alternatively you need to choose somebody

who knows enough about IT so that he or she can be completely sure of what he or she is saying. If you find a long serving, articulate and persuasive senior IT manager (does such a beast exist?) you will probably be on to a winner!

Once you have established your project management structure, the project should follow the same sort of structure however large or small your organization. Figure 2 outlines each of the steps you need to go through – each step is expanded later in this book.

Following Figure 2 is a series of slides that can be used in presentations to management in this context – you may find them helpful in making your decisions!

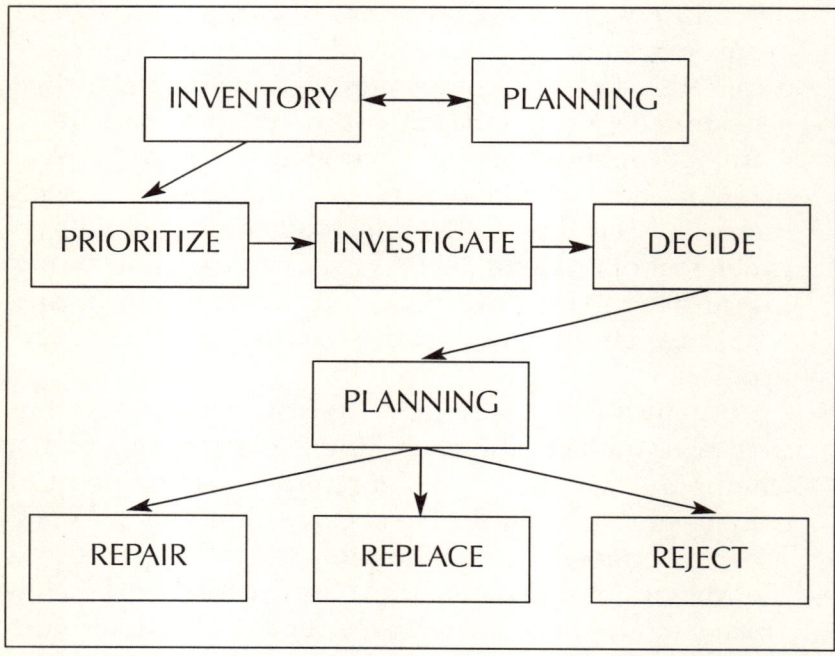

Figure 2   *The Year 2000 project structure*

Project Management Issues

➤ Project is crucial for your organization

➤ Project has a completely immovable end date...

➤ So –

➤ Choose your leader/co-ordinator with care!

➤ Make sure that you have high-level backing

Department or Organization

➤ Is IT organized and managed departmentally?

➤ Then you need a liaison group

➤ Is it central?

➤ Then you need a liaison group!

Figure 3 *Slides that may be used in presentations to management*

Choose Your Leader

➤ Find someone influential

➤ Find someone trustworthy

➤ Decide – manager/co-ordinator

➤ Give them sufficient authority

➤ Tell everyone else!

Plan

➤ Don't plan ahead!
(Plan Backwards!)

➤ Be realistic (again)

➤ Prioritize ruthlessly

➤ Discuss with all interested parties

Figure 3 *continued*

Planning Backwards

- ➤ Set definite milestones eg 01/04/99 for financial systems
- ➤ Work backwards to set acceptance date start, etc
- ➤ If you miss a milestone – don't replan, re-think!!

Prioritize

➤ Organizational priorities

➤ Need to get everyone on board

➤ You *will* tread on toes!!

➤ Everything must be considered – think the unthinkable!!

Figure 3 *continued*

THE TECHNICAL ISSUES

Lessons Learnt

➤ Critical requirement for an organizational champion

➤ Must have dedicated liaison groups

➤ Need to see the difference between this and other projects

➤ Use a timeline!

Figure 3 *continued*

Inventory

Make a detailed list of all those parts of your operation that could be affected!

One of the many difficulties associated with the Year 2000 problem is that the time and resources necessary to resolve it bring no benefit apart from the ability to keep going. Ironically, the very first step in the process is the one that can bring you the most long-term benefit. You cannot start investigating the problem until you know what you have got.

No one would argue that having a full, detailed and up to date inventory of IT assets was not an ideal – few could boast that they had such a thing. Compiling an inventory, however, is a completely necessary first step in any Year 2000 project.

ELEMENTS OF THE INVENTORY

An inventory is a working document compiled for one, or many, purposes and is not an end in itself. The information you put into an inventory is the information you want to get out of it. Below we will cover what is needed for the

THE TECHNICAL ISSUES

Year 2000 project – you may consider adding other information which you might need for projects in the future.

FORMAT

The format of your inventory is entirely up to you, but there are one or two basic principles to be remembered.

- It must be easy to access. Don't store it on the hard disk of one PC unless this is all you have. Keep it where as many people as possible can update it. Always keep a back-up and always keep two hard copies, one off-site. More than one organization has had a server and PCs stolen and found that the only copy of the inventory has gone with them.
- It must be easy to update. An out-of-date inventory is slightly less useful than a broken watch, which is accurate at least once a day. Your inventory must be easy and quick to update or maintaining it will fall to the bottom of the priority list.
- It must be flexible. Unless you want to keep endless different inventories for different types of equipment, your inventory must be flexible enough to hold different details for different types of equipment, and to hold new details which were not foreseen at the time of setting up the inventory. There are few things more frustrating than trying to enter a PC into an inventory, being asked to enter the number of a 5¼" disk drive, which is now obsolete, and not being able to enter a CD-ROM drive.
- It must be 'owned'. Some may not consider this to be important, but it is probable that, unless your inventory is owned by an individual who takes responsibility for the integrity of the data in it, the quality will not be maintained. Technical staff are notoriously bad at administration and it is difficult to integrate it into their

processes. In order to ensure this, an individual or an individual team must be responsible for the function.

Once these principles are established the actual format of the inventory matters little. There are plenty of products on the market which compile inventories especially of PC hardware and software. As an alternative, you could produce your own using any proprietary spreadsheet or database. One thing which may affect your choice could be whether you wish to use it for totalling numbers of PCs, etc which will mean you need to use a program capable of doing calculations. One recommended option is to use a table in a word processor into which you can add as many textual comments as you like. From this you can import information into a spreadsheet for sorting and calculation. This approach allows great flexibility while still keeping the inventory easy to read and update. An example is given in Figure 4.

As you can see the inventory does not have to be complex – clarity is all-important! Whatever format you choose for the inventory you will need to record details of your hardware, software, embedded chips and contracts.

HARDWARE

You need to record sufficient details about your IT hardware to be able to talk sensibly about it to your suppliers. At a minimum this needs to include:

- your own tag/ID number
- make
- model
- serial number
- date purchased
- supplier

Systems Inventory

Prepared By: AN Other
Prepared on: 21st May 1996

This inventory lists all systems owned by the XXXX

Systems Supported by YYY:

System Name	Owner	Breakdown	Comments	Users	Location	Priority
Property Ordering System	Property	Property Server1 Currently running AN Operating system version 001 – will be running version 2.X after end of upgrade project Y. Application written in Language 1 Interface programs with mainframe **Contingency – Paper based system**	Currently thought to be able to cope with all problems all dates were specified as having 4 character year fields – However should be fully tested	Property Dept Payments	Machine Room	Critical Business System – statutory obligations
Transport System	Transport-tation	No longer being used properly. Stand alone on A. Person's computer **Contingency – not required**	Diskette upload to General Ledger which may no longer be required in the year 2000 **check with A. Manager**	Transport	1st floor B Block	No longer required
Time Recording System	Clerical Section	Package Supplier - ???? Database ??? **Contingency – none as yet**	No support information	All Depts	All offices	Critical Business System – Investigation must be given priority

Figure 4 *Systems inventory*

- BIOS and date (if a PC)
- repair history details (if available)
- location
- maintenance/DR contracts
- owner
- user
- comments about which functions the equipment is used for.

SOFTWARE

You need to record the details which will enable you to talk sensibly to your supplier or support company about your software. There is, however, another aspect to software – and that is data, and your inventory must record details about this. So the minimum you need to record here is:

- location (ie where installed)
- program/system name
- version
- supplier
- main users/owner
- support company
- main files accessed
- interfaces

NB – You need to record details of all software including operating systems, databases, spreadsheets, word processors and applications.

CONTRACTS

You may be surprised to see these appearing in an inventory – but contracts of all sorts are just as important as the other items in the inventory, as they will be affected by the Millennium and they all need investigating. (See Chapter 6 on 'Investigation' and Chapter 9 below on the case for a contractual audit).

So you need, as a minimum, to record the details of all your major contracts for supplies and services, and you need to record:

- name of contractor
- purpose of contract
- expiry date
- client manager.

EMBEDDED CHIPS

In many ways, these are the most problematical. One of the complications of the embedded chip area is that you may not know what contains a chip and what doesn't. You need to record the details of absolutely everything that you think might possibly contain a chip – you can always delete items once you have established that they do not. If you have a large organization, use your staff to help you gather the data, using questionnaires as in the model in Appendix B to gather your information. The details which you need to record are very much like those for hardware, so:

- tag/ID number
- make
- model
- serial number
- date purchased
- supplier
- maintenance contract
- location
- purpose

- owner
- repair history details – this is especially important with embedded chips – repairs sometimes mean replacing the very chips which cause the problems and if this is not recorded investigative action can be tricky.

COMMON ITEMS

There are two pieces of information which are common to all the items on your inventory – future use and contingency plans.

Future Use

Among your inventory items there may well be items which you are planning to replace. As long as you are *absolutely sure* that they will be replaced, then you can mark this on your inventory and take no further action, but there are some points you need to think about before you make your decision.

- If the item is business critical it would be wise to investigate it anyway, just in case something stops your plan. That 'something' may be the Year 2000 project itself which may well take resources from other projects.
- Take care if you need to look at historical data from a system. When you replace a system you sometimes need to keep historical data. Don't forget that you may not be able to if the system is not compliant. Also you may not be able to restore from back copies, so don't rely on these either.
- It is probably safer to investigate the item anyway, even if you take no action unless you have to.
- Replacement systems also need to be checked for compliance.

Contingency Plans

For each of your items you need to formulate a contingency plan. The item may not be compliant; you may not be able to make it compliant in time; you may miss problems which crop up after you think that it is completely compliant. You therefore need to formulate a plan to cover any or all of these risks. Again, there are some points to consider.

- You will need to tailor your plans as a result of your investigations (see Chapter 6 below). These may point to a failure date earlier than you expected, or a failure in a specific part of a system. Make general plans at first and refine them later.
- Don't make your plans too complex – you need to make sure that everyone will understand them and that they will work.
- Don't plan to use another item by way of contingency unless you are sure that that item is compliant!
- Don't rely on existing disaster recovery plans unless you are sure that everything that you will use in them is compliant. This applies particularly to system and hardware disaster recovery plans. These usually rely on replacing like with like, which would not be a good solution in the case of something failing because of Millennium problems.
- Make sure that you communicate your plans. Most contingency plans are heavily reliant on people and you must be sure that everyone who needs to know about them, does know about them, and that these people will be around at the time they will be needed, especially over the Millennium New Year holiday.

Take a simple example from the education arena. Many schools have central heating systems which are becoming elderly and may have had several repairs over the years. It may therefore be difficult to establish any compliance information about them, and a contingency plan will be needed. This could be as follows.

- Establish whether the heating system has any sort of manual override.
- Ensure that a technician/caretaker will be available to check the system on 1st January to establish the situation. His/her role is to switch the heating on if there is a manual override or report to the head teacher if there is not.
- Book some portable heating equipment in case the heating will not come on.
- As a final contingency, make plans with the school governors to keep children away from the school in case this is necessary.

A simple plan, but one depending on the headteacher, caretaker, governors and parents all being informed, and substitute equipment being booked, if possible, in advance.

Once you have compiled your inventory, make it someone's responsibility to own and make it an integral part of your change management procedures. It is absolutely crucial to your project's success, and you need to treat it as such.

Planning

Make a plan to deal with the problems you face!

While you are in the process of completing your inventory, you must begin your planning. Experienced project managers will wonder why there is a separate chapter on planning – but the Year 2000 project is quite different from any other sort of project.

Most IT projects, in fact most projects of any sort, tend to run beyond the allotted time. This project cannot do so. The end date is completely immovable and may, in fact, have to be moved forward as investigations show that programs may fail in advance of the Millennium (see 'Investigation' in Chapter 6). On top of this, each investigation may show new problems, unforeseen errors, and, of course, IT systems you didn't know you had. It has been said that the Millennium is like an onion – the more layers you peel off the more you find, and the more you find the more you cry.

What this means is that you have to be totally flexible within completely constrained boundaries. Of course, normal project management techniques apply here as much as with any other project – but there are some techniques which you need to adopt which are specific to this particular project.

PLANNING BACKWARDS

A piece of advice for all readers to bear in mind and which is valid whenever you start your Year 2000 project is DON'T PLAN AHEAD – PLAN BACKWARDS.

What is meant is this – when managing a normal project you work out and plan your project, and document the agreed timetable. During your project, if the timetable slips, or new requirements emerge, you re-plan your project and usually agree on a new planned end date. With a Year 2000 project, this is impossible. Whilst other projects may usually have fixed end dates, although this is frequently inconvenient, the end date can be moved or contingency plans put into place. However, the Year 2000 project is an exacerbated version of these. What you need to do with the Year 2000 project is to acknowledge the immovable end date and manage back from it. Like all project planning, it is best kept simple. So, take a piece of paper and draw a line on it. Put 1st January, 2000 at one end of it, and the current date at the other end – that represents the time which you have available to you. Now you need to put onto the line the known critical milestone dates. These will be a mixture of those driven by the technology – ie 1st April, 1999 when many financial systems will fail – those driven by the organization, ie dates at which you need to get information to those preparing the budgets, etc, and those which are based on your experience of your organization.

This latter needs expanding – at some point along the timeline you need to have reached a view on how many PCs you will need to replace. Working back then from 1st January, 2000, you can work out when you need to start the process to achieve your target date. The length of time will clearly depend on the amount of resource available, the geographical nature of your organization and optimum times for replacing operational PCs. Another example is acceptance testing – if you are having, for instance, to replace a major financial system, your experience may tell you that you need at least twelve months for testing and error correction. A financial system probably needs to be compliant by 1st April, 1999 – so you really need to have started already.

You should find that your line is quickly filled up and, bearing in mind the resources available to you, you can start filling up the detail. What you *cannot* do is to move any of the critical milestones.

Having drawn up your timeline plan you need to allow it to dominate the life of your project. Check your progress against your timeline every week – tick off what you have achieved. If something does slip you cannot re-plan your timeline because the dates are immovable. The only options available to you are these:

- bring in extra resources to get you back on target, or
- according to your priority list either drop this part of the project and invoke your contingency, or drop something else.

This is all basic project planning – but project planning very much focused on dates and priority. Figure 5 gives an idea of what you need to do – none of it is difficult or complex! Obviously the dates have now passed but the figure should give you some idea of how to tackle the planning process.

MAKING DECISIONS

This is where the flexibility needs to come in. Again, like all projects, unexpected findings will come out of your investigations and unexpected problems will arise. Because of the limited time available, you do not have enough time for the sort of decision-making practices which you might use in an ordinary project. You may be working with third parties with their own project timetables. You may be reliant

THE TECHNICAL ISSUES

Millennium Overall Time Line Plan

Jan 1997	Apr 1997	Jun 1997	Sept 1997	Apr 1998	Sept 1998	Jan 1999	Apr 1999	9th September 1999 (09/09/1999) 9/9/9 or 9999	Jan 2000
1. Detailed Change Control Log to be run from now on. This is to ensure that all changes/ enhancements are millennium compliant. 2. Monthly progress reports and meetings required throughout the process.	1. High level planning complete 2. System inventories complete.	1. Detailed planning complete. 2. Top level system priorities proposed, including business criticality and key systems in terms of failure date.	1. Review estimates. 2. System priorities agreed by directors and group leaders	1. Review estimates. 2. Major wide review. Develop contingency plans. 3. Financial systems ready for user testing. Forms and procedures updated. 4. Fully compliant mainframe. 5. Fully compliant platforms for non M/F systems eg Unix PC.	1. Review estimates. 2. Test PCs and identify required upgrades.	1. All non financial systems ready for UAT testing, including forms and procedures. 2. Fully compliant test beds set up, for non financial systems.	1. Financial systems fully compliant. (This is a target – the minimum being that systems which process years must be compliant). 2. Review estimates.	1. Check all backup, archiving systems and file expiry dates. 2. Check all security systems and system modules. 3. Check all sorting code specifically.	All systems fully compliant.

Figure 5 *Project planning*

on strict and restricted testing windows. You may have consultants or contract resources on time-limited contracts. Thus you need to make decisions very quickly indeed and be flexible about your working practices.

How you do this is very dependent on the size and type of your organization. If you are a 'one person band' or a very small organization with no in-house computing facility, you need to ensure that you draw up a contract with a third party which is as flexible as possible. You can go for an 'outcome' related contract as long as you are confident that the contractors are flexible enough themselves to adapt to whatever unexpected events occur. If you have several systems being amended by a single third party, it might be better to go for a volume type contract where you can determine priorities yourself. Whichever you go for you need to ensure that your contract has sufficient monitoring and review to enable you to build in the flexibility that you need. If you are a large organization which is using mainly in-house resource for your project, you need to exploit the management within your own organization to ensure quick decision making and flexibility. Below are points you need to remember.

Communication

Don't build up a complex matrix of project meetings through which it is impossible to navigate quickly. You need swift communication lines, with especially clear lines of responsibility. Take an example from the mainframe world. A particular project was to be managed in phases. At the end of each phase a particular system would be copied into production, fully Millennium compliant. Each phase involved changes to database software and systems software as well as applications, and the project was planned to run over six phases in six successive months. Unfortunately, after the end of the first phase it was discovered that the first system, once upgraded, could not interface with the others. A quick, critical but very risky decision had to be made: *All* the systems had to be copied into production at the same time. Some had not been tested thoroughly – some of the programming was scarcely completed.

- The main processes had already been put into place for moving quickly.
- Emergency communications with users were agreed.
- The staff required to make decisions were agreed and were given authority to make those decisions.
- The authority to make the final decision to go ahead was given to one person and everyone understood the situation.

A simple, but successful, process.

Understanding

In order to facilitate this sort of flexibility of communication, you need to ensure that everyone understands the nature of the project and what it is for. If they do not, you will have enormous difficulties when you have to make swift and sometimes unpopular decisions. But this understanding needs to go further than just the project team. *All* the staff in your organization need to understand the priority and criticality of this project. If you can get the message across to the staff, it has enormous advantages because you can tap their knowledge and experience:

- they know which systems support the organization's priorities
- they know which 'embedded' system items they use to do their own jobs
- they will understand why they need to make time for tasks such as testing

- they will understand the project's priorities.

The member of staff whose working day is spent using a system which is deemed to be low priority will not be won over unless he or she understands the 'big picture' in this way.

Planning needs to suit your organization – you need to be flexible, you need to communicate. But you must remember:

- to check your progress against your timeline every two weeks
- to re-prioritize before you re-plan
- to be prepared to make quick, possibly unpopular, possibly risky, but critical decisions.

Prioritize/Investigate/ Decide

Right – I've got my inventory and plan, but what do I do now?

You will not be able to make all of your systems perfectly compliant. Unless you are reading this book simply to consolidate what you have already done or you are a very small enterprise or all your equipment is very new and you are very lucky, you are probably too late to inventory, investigate, and replace or repair all your systems. This means that what you must do is prioritize, and prioritize ruthlessly.

PRIORITIZATION

The first thing that you need to do is to decide the criteria which you are going to use to prioritize. It is unlikely that you have very much unused equipment or surplus software, so you must think very clearly about what is really critical for your business. The sort of things which you need to think about are very straightforward, but some can be easily overlooked. Any organization, large or small needs to give priority to:

THE TECHNICAL ISSUES

- any functions which have any Health and Safety implications. These are likely especially to be embedded chip systems, but could also be computer hardware and software, and could also be contracts for such things as cleaning services. You must look at these as a priority in view of the obvious risk of endangering the lives of your employees, and the public, but also to prevent yourself being open to litigation
- any other functions which might expose your business to litigation under any other legislation. This could relate to statutory duties in the case of local authorities, or, for instance, trading standards legislation in the case of sell-by dates
- programs and equipment which support functions without which your business will fail *and* for which there is no possible manual substitute
- within these you need to identify which will fail first.

The first two points are particular to your own organization, although some items will be the same for all, such as fire alarms. You need to seek advice from your organization's Health and Safety Officer or from the Health and Safety Executive. Similarly, your own lawyers will be able to tell you which of your business's functions are critical from a legal point of view, and you will need to establish which technologies support these functions. This process may throw up some surprises for you. In many public authorities, for example, you may think that the financial programs are the most important because of local government legislation, and the general ledger certainly dominates most businesses. In fact it is far more likely that the social services or education systems need to take priority.

It is in the third category where you will need to be particularly careful to identify the priority systems. Some programs or equipment may appear to be critical to the business, but can easily be replaced by manual procedures.

Take, for example, your electronic mail system. It may be the most heavily used system which you have but, unless you use it to communicate with third parties for essential business use, you can replace it with the telephone (as long as you are sure that your voice system is compliant!), fax (ditto!) or paper mail. Thus your very heavily used mail system may well be a lesser priority than your fire alarm or critical supplier contract.

Once you have established your priority criteria, don't be too complex. Clarity is the most important thing here. It's important to have a very clear picture of your priorities – don't try to write your next year's business plans at the same time!

INVESTIGATION

Once you have prioritized your systems, you need to start investigating their compliance status. Although this may appear to be the major part of your Year 2000 project, and may well be the largest in terms of numbers of hours, it is in many ways the most straightforward. Once you have compiled and prioritized your inventory, what you must do is to be completely systematic in your investigations. The different types of inventory item – hardware/software, embedded chips and contracts, all require a different type of investigative technique but the process has some fundamental common principles.

- Be completely systematic and stick to your priorities.
- Don't make assumptions about which systems do and do not process dates. A system or embedded chip item which does not obviously process dates may, in the case of the system, have dates in the security processing, and, in the case of the embedded chip item, hold servicing dates.

THE TECHNICAL ISSUES

- Keep investigating/asking until you get a definite, and substantiated answer.
- Don't make decisions about how to deal with the item at this stage – they might be the wrong ones, as you cannot be completely informed until you have completed your investigations.
- Make sure that you record the date at which you think the equipment or system will fail – this will help you with your priorities.

In reality, you may have to start making decisions before you have finished your investigations for each item – as long as you deal with your priority items first, this is fine – but try not to make decisions about items until you have sufficient information for those decisions to be informed ones, otherwise you may make serious mistakes!

Advice, Consultancy and Software Tools

Before you start, you may want to consider using the services of one of the many consultancy firms advertising in the computer press, and/or some of the software tools available. Because these also cover the replace/repair stage of the project, they will be dealt with under a separate heading below. However, beware that the contract which you negotiate with the service provider provides you with the guarantees which you need. In this context, see the comments on Solution Provider Agreements in Chapter 9.

Hardware

All computers, from PCs to mainframes, contain microcode which stores the current date. This is stored inside the computer and, although you may not be aware of it on a day to day basis, it is passed through to any programs running on the computer. This code, however, can and in many cases will report the wrong date, passing through a date in 1900, or a date in 1980. In some cases, however, the machine will be unable to cope and will not complete its start-up sequence. You need to discover whether your hardware will be affected like this.

The primary source of information on hardware must be your supplier and/or your support company. For mainframe computers and for large or custom-built servers, you will need to enquire about each individual machine as they tend to be unique, using a letter like that in Appendix B. Your support company/supplier should know your machines well enough to be able to give you a definitive answer for each one.

For smaller servers and personal computers you probably need to take a different approach. The mainstream suppliers are publishing information on the Internet (see for example, the database at *www.weblaw.co.uk*) or in the computing press which gives you details concerning compliance based on the BIOS version and date. You will need to record this information for each machine you have, and compare it with the statements from the suppliers. If the machines are not badged, but have been built by yourself or a third party, you still need to record the BIOS version and date, and then seek information from the BIOS manufacturer. Whichever way you investigate, you need to record your findings against each machine on your inventory. You also need to think about the following:

- don't make unfounded assumptions – machines you bought very recently may not necessarily be compliant. Also two machines bought on the same day from the same supplier can have different BIOS versions, one compliant and one not
- if you can't find out any information – fear the worst!

The BIOS clock is a good indication of compliance but is not

THE TECHNICAL ISSUES

the whole story. In order to be absolutely sure you need to check the CMOS and the Real Time Clock. If you have more than a very few PCs, it is wise to buy one of the many software products available to help you. These vary in price and functionality and, in essence, you get what you pay for, but you should be able to purchase a product on a site licence for less than £200. Many of these also offer you software 'fix' – see below in 'Repair'. You need to be careful when using these products, so make sure that you read the instructions very carefully. There is also a problem with the way some manufacturers have achieved compliance. This depends on the computer being switched on over midnight of 31st December, 1999 and calculating 1st January, 2000 from there – tested today the machine appears not to be compliant. This is a good reason for using both questions to the supplier and software tests for determining compliance.

There are one or two other points to remember.

- Do not try testing any computers by starting them up and changing the date yourself, unless you have absolutely no alternative. This can be an extremely risky process because...
  - your software may expire if it contains embedded licence dates. Some software sets a flag to say that the licence has expired. When you restart the machine with the current date the flag will still be set and you will not be able to run the software again
  - if you have any software which automatically deletes files of a certain age you may lose files which the system thinks are older than they actually are
  - the system may refuse to start up and you may not be able to recover it.

A good tip which many organizations have adopted is to have stickers printed – red for non-compliant, green for compliant. This has the double effect of backing up your inventory and also reminding all your budget managers that they have a problem (or not!).

Other items of hardware (scanners, printers, etc) are much trickier. Some printers are almost mini-computers and have sophisticated software associated with them. You need to write to your supplier/support company for information.

Software

Your approach towards software will depend very much on what type of software you are running and the availability of in-house IT skills within your company. The bottom line is the same whatever your set-up. You need to find out whether your software has any date-dependent processing contained in the code, and whether that processing can cope with the century change. It is a common misconception to believe that only certain programs will be affected by the Year 2000, or that only mainframe programs will go wrong. This is completely wrong – *any* code can contain date-dependent processing and needs to be investigated. There are, however, different approaches for different types of software, and these types can be split into the following categories: Operating Systems, Processing Software, and Application Software.

Operating Systems

These can be classified as the software which 'drives' and 'controls' the computer. Examples of these would be MS DOS and Windows in the PC world, UNIX, Netware and MVS in the mid-range and mainframe world. All these contain date-dependent processing. As a computer user, or even as a programmer, you may be able to test whether the operating systems are Year 2000 compliant – you cannot change them if they are not. So for this class of software you need to rely on the manufacturer to supply you with the information you need for your investigation. There are

THE TECHNICAL ISSUES

plenty of places to look for information – many web sites have lists of operating systems, versions, and details of their compliance. The best route is to start with the web site of the software manufacturer. You can also ask you software maintenance company, and facilities management company if you have one.

You may find that manufacturers are only prepared to give you compliance statements with a 'caveat' – that is they will only guarantee their software compliant if it runs on compliant hardware. This is perfectly reasonable. In most cases the operating system takes its date from the BIOS of the computer on which it is running – if this is incorrect, the operating system's date will also be incorrect.

If you discover that the version you are running is not compliant or you are uncertain, you need to ask some detailed questions – an example of a questionnaire you can use is given in Appendix B. If you find that you need to upgrade to a later version, you need to find out:

- whether the new system requires greater machine capacity (more memory, disk space, a faster processor, etc)
- is the upgrade a major one, or just a small change? If a major one you may need to consider user/technical training, etc
- can the supplier give you details of how the upgrade will affect programs running under the operating system? Some of your existing application programs or processing software may not run under the new version
- will the upgrade cost you any money? This may depend on whether or not you have a maintenance agreement for the software. But some companies issuing only minor upgrades may let you have the upgrade free, or it may be issued as code which can be downloaded over the Internet.

You will need to record all these details to help you decide what action to take.

Processing Software

This is a rather curious title, but is intended to cover all the 'systems' software which is provided either to process data, or to allow you to code your own programs to do so. Into this category come databases, spreadsheets, word processors, code generators and compilers. These, like operating systems, are not usually changed by the user but come as packaged software. The approach to them is exactly the same as that for operating systems – you need to find out the information that you require from manufacturers, suppliers and any maintenance company you might deal with. There is, however, an extra question you need to ask – if you do have to upgrade the software to make it compliant you need to find out whether the new version will run under your existing or upgraded operating system.

Application Software

This heading includes the software which is particular to your way of working. Typically these are specific systems written for a particular task – a general ledger, payroll system, time recording, machinery control systems, mapping software, etc. Many are packaged, but many are 'bespoke', that is to say written to your particular requirements either by a software house, or by in-house resource. Included in this category are those database and spreadsheet systems written by computer users using the processing software detailed above.

In many ways, this can be the most complex category of software to deal with.

Packaged, 'off the shelf' software needs to be dealt with exactly like operating systems, and processing software.

THE TECHNICAL ISSUES

But, if you need to upgrade, there is another question to ask – do you need to upgrade the processing software on which the application is based? If this is confusing, consider your IT as a series of layers:

- hardware
- operating system
- processing software
- applications software and...
- data (we will look at this later).

They are all mutually dependent, and you need to ensure that you do not consider upgrading any one of them, without considering the others.

If your software is bespoke, it is probably unique to you, and therefore you will need to ensure that it is investigated carefully to determine its compliance. It does not matter whether the software was written in-house. Do not make assumptions yourself about whether the code has any date processing – it may not appear to have, but could well use dates for file handling or security.

There is one particular question you need to ask for processing software and application software – and that is, if the software is compliant, how has it been made so? The reason for this is a technique called 'windowing'. One way to make software compliant is to code the program so that, if it encounters a year ending '00' to '30' (say) it assumes this is 2000, or 2030, but any year above this is treated as 1931, etc. This is a perfectly valid way of making software compliant *but* only if the data you will be processing allows it. It would not be suitable for programs processing dates of birth – these may require the ability to process dates from the 1800s!

Data

Although this is not really software it needs to be considered in the same way. While looking at your application programs you need to consider the data they are processing – if the data has been entered with two character years, the program will not be able to assume to which century they refer. Moreover, if the program is made compliant, it will make an assumption about a year entered as '00' which may be incorrect. You also need to investigate any data interfaces used by your programs – either those going out from your systems to others, or those coming in. If you identify any interfaces of this sort you must contact the owners of the systems to, or from which yours are interfacing and ensure that you agree on the format of the data in the interface.

Lastly don't forget input forms. If your forms are pre-printed with '19' in the year, and this is punched into the system, all your compliance work will be wasted!

Embedded Chips

This is probably the trickiest area you will have to deal with. It is difficult enough to identify which embedded chip systems you have yourself – it is much more difficult to find out whether they are compliant or not. As in the case of hardware and software, you are very much in the hands of the suppliers/maintainers of your equipment. You need to contact them with as much information as you have, and include, especially, details of any repairs made to your equipment. Sometimes these repairs can change the chip as well – this means that the equipment is not to the specification that it was originally, and the supplier may not be able to give you correct information. Again you may find help on the World Wide Web, and also from the professional organizations, particularly the Institute of Electrical Engineers. In some cases you can investigate yourself – but take care! As with computer hardware, changing the date to test the compliance status could be dangerous – and many embedded chip systems cannot be backed up. There are already stories of people changing dates on, for instance, central heating clocks, finding they are not compliant, and then finding that they cannot be started up again in the current year.

Contracts

This section should be read in conjunction with the section on the 'Case for a Contract Audit' in Chapter 9. We will focus here on two aspects of contracts. The contractors themselves, and their compliance status – and the contract renewal date.

Each of your contractors, however small their business, should be running their own Year 2000 project. They will probably run some computers themselves, or use systems with embedded chips. At the very least, they will themselves be dependent on suppliers. You need to ensure that your own contractors/suppliers are not going to go out of business because of the Millennium. You therefore need to be writing to them to ensure that they have a project running and to find out how they are progressing. You need to keep writing until you are happy with the answer you get – and you need to ask for frequent progress reports if the contract is a critical one.

The issue of the contract end date is a rather different one. During 1999 many companies will be tightly stretched trying to deal with the Millennium problem, and may not have the resource to fulfil all their contractual requirements. It is also a possibility that some may choose to go out of business rather than spend the money required to put their systems right. The implications of this are that you may find it difficult to renew contracts which are due to expire in 1999, and you may find it even more difficult to find new contractors then. It is important to investigate all your contracts now, and if you find any due to expire in 1999 see whether you can negotiate extra time, or renew them early.

DECISIONS

You should now have an inventory full of information about each item, and prioritized according to your business requirements. Now you must begin to decide how you are going to approach each item based on what you have discovered about it.

Compliant Items

Even if you think, or have been assured, that items are compliant you still have some decisions to make about them. The most important is probably to ask yourself whether you can trust the assurances you have been given, or whether you need to test the item anyway. You need to consider the following when making your decision.

- Is the item business-critical? If it is you probably need to check out the information or test the item unless you are absolutely confident that the information can be trusted.
- Can the item be tested? More about testing later, but with some items, especially embedded chip equipment, there may be no method available to test it.
- Are you happy with the technique adopted to achieve compliance? There are basically three ways to achieve compliance:
- use four-character years – the system already uses four character years
- 'windowing', as described above, where you code the program to make assumptions about the century based on the year
- coding round. This involves coding statements which supply the century if a date is stored as two characters, usually linked with reading in a table of valid dates before the program starts.

THE TECHNICAL ISSUES

Each of these techniques is valid, but may be inappropriate. You need to decide whether the technique used fits the data you have. Relevant questions in this context include:

- does the system need to change any of its interfaces?
- does it need to change, although itself compliant, because of other changes, eg changes in operating system?
- do the input forms need changing?

As a result of the answers to these questions you may find that you need to do some work on the system even if it is already compliant.

Non-compliant Items

Once you have established that an item is not, or probably is not, compliant you have some tough decisions to make. You really only have three choices: Repair, Replace, or Reject. The type of technology helps you choose between the first and the second – the third choice can be much harder.

Repair

The approach to this decision depends on the type of item you are looking at.

Hardware

It is possible to 'repair' computer hardware to make it compliant – that is you can buy hardware and software fixes to make the microcode compliant, or to bypass it. These include extra cards to put into the machine, 'flash' fixes to change the microcode itself, or programs which cut in when the machine starts up to change the date to a compliant version. All these can work – but they do need to be treated with care. If, for instance, your application program takes its date from the Real Time Clock, the software fix will cut in too late. Alternatively all these fixes may be dependent on the network, so fixing the PC will not help. The software fixes, on the other hand, can easily be deleted in error.

You need to make your decision based on the criticality of the item and the timescale. If the piece of hardware is business-critical it would seem unwise to depend on such a fix – if, however, the item is not business-critical it might be a good choice. In the case of PCs, where many are subject to a 'rolling' plan of replacement, you could choose to use the fix if the machine has not been replaced before the start of the Millennium. Always remember that if the machine will start up after 1st January, 2000, you may not need to repair it at all. If, say, it is stand alone and only used very rarely maybe it does not matter – but make sure that you affix a sticker indicating that it is not compliant to ensure that it is not moved to a different, and more critical, location!

Software

Repair is a very real option for software, but has one prerequisite – you must be able to access the source code. Although this would seem to be self-evident, many organizations have found that they no longer have the source code for some of their most critical systems, and others that the programs are written in old-fashioned languages which can no longer be maintained by their staff. This can also be the case for software houses, and, unless you have an escrow agreement in place, you may not be able to force them to hand the code over. In this context, see the section on 'Object Code, Source Code and Escrow' in Chapter 9. Thus, even if repair might seem to be a good decision, it may not be possible. If, however, you can access the source code, these are the things you need to think about when considering whether to repair the software.

THE TECHNICAL ISSUES

- Availability of skills. If your system was written in-house, and you can access the source code, you may not have access to resource with the necessary skills to amend it for you. The most obvious solution to this is to employ more permanent staff, or contractors, to do the job for you. But this has a price-tag attached – and it is not a small one! Staff skilled in the older, 'legacy' languages are now at a premium and may be unavailable. (Incidentally, if you do have in-house resource available with the right skills you need to remember that they, also, are at a premium! Many companies are considering offering loyalty bonuses to staff who stay past the Millennium).
- The code may be so old that it cannot be repaired or, when repaired, cannot run under the newer operating systems. This can be a real problem, especially for those companies with mainframe systems. The Millennium compliant operating systems may support the old application programs, but not the language compilers which are needed to amend them. In some cases, a change in operating system may impose the need for changes to all the software running under it.
- The life of the system. If the system is old and creaky, or simply no longer fulfilling your requirements, you *may* still have the opportunity to replace it rather than repair it. But take care before you make this decision! Once you have started the process of replacing it, you may not have time to change your mind. If the system is critical, repairing it is probably the safest option, then you could start to replace it, but retaining the repaired system by way of contingency.
- Timescale. This almost contradicts the above point – but still has to be borne in mind! You need to consider whether you have sufficient time to repair your system. As time marches on you may not have time to repair the system successfully, and you may need to fall back on your contingency plan.

- Compliance technique. This refers back to the three different techniques referred to above under 'Compliant Items'. You need to consider whether it is possible to repair the system with one of these techniques, and still leave it processing data appropriately.

Embedded Chips

If you can locate the chip, and replace it without detriment to the rest of the construction, then you can repair the item. This is a simple statement, but is more difficult to put into practice! Again, you are completely reliant on your supplier or maintenance company to inform you, and probably to do the repair for you. Your decision needs to be based, once again, on the criticality of the system, its age, and the cost to replace it. If the system is critical, especially if there are any health and safety implications, then, unless it is very new, you probably need to replace it if you can afford to. This may be the only course of action if you cannot find out any information about its compliance status. If you do choose to repair it, you need to ensure that you have a contingency plan ready.

Replace (or Upgrade)

The approach to this decision is the same whatever type of item you are considering. In many cases, replacement may be the only course of action open to you, and this is almost certainly the case for much of the packaged software run by many organizations. You need to consider the following.

- Is there a replacement? There is no point in deciding to replace an item unless you are sure that there is a replacement, or an upgrade, available.
- Does the upgrade, or replacement system, do the same job? In the case of most packaged software you do not have any involvement in its specification – a new release

THE TECHNICAL ISSUES

may work quite differently from the old one, and may not fulfil your requirements.
- Does the upgrade, or replacement system, run on your hardware/operating system/processing software?
- Will the upgrade, or replacement system, require any user training?
- Will the upgrade, or replacement system, read your data? Almost certainly it will not and you may need to run a conversion program. A special word of warning here – you may not be able to read any archived data, so consider printing or microficheing this if it is essential.
- Have you got time to upgrade or replace? Major upgrades require a large amount of implementation and testing so, once again, you need to have your contingency plan ready if you have any doubts about your ability to finish in time. This also goes for contracts – if you decide to re-tender a contract because the present contractor is showing no signs of progress towards being Millennium compliant, do not forget how long this process can take!
- Are you sure that the replacement, or upgrade, is compliant? Do not assume that it is – you need to be sure!

Reject (or Do Nothing!)

There are three reasons why you might reject an item, or decide not to do anything about its lack of compliance.

- The item will not be required. Think very carefully before making this decision. If the item is not required *now*, then take it off your inventory! If it is still required, are you sure that it will function for as long as you need it? Do not forget that some programs will fail on 1st January, 1999 – are you sure that you will not require the item after that? If you do not require it because it is being replaced then make sure that the project dealing with that replacement is aware of the timescales.

- The item cannot be repaired or replaced within the timetable or budget. You need to recognize this as a possibility – some of your lower priority items may have to 'fall off' your list and be left until after the Millennium, while you invoke your contingency plans until they can be dealt with.
- The lack of compliance does not matter. This is a real issue. If the lack of compliance is purely cosmetic – eg printing out dates as '00' – but does not affect the accuracy of the processing, this can be dealt with at a later date. Don't be panicked into thinking that you must deal with everything – perhaps you need to consider documents going out to your customers, but internal documents probably do not matter!

Once you have made your decision, record it on your inventory, and, if it could possibly be contentious, record your reasons for making it. Then you must communicate your decisions as widely as you can including the reasons for making them. This is important if you are going to keep your staff on board, and is very much the same issue as was discussed above in Chapter 3. In this, as in everything, your staff members are your most important assets and you need to make sure that they are on your side. This is the point at which you need to have staff awareness sessions if you have not had them before – or continue them if you have started already.

More planning

Be prepared for shocks – and plan how to cope with them!

You are now in possession of a large amount of information about your inventory items, and have decided what action you need to take for each one. Now you have a planning exercise to complete. At this point the Year 2000 project is much like any other – you need to estimate the length of time required for each task you need to do and map it onto the available time and resource accessible to you. If you have a large inventory, one of the proprietary project management software packages would be useful, although they can be complex and it would be wise not to choose this particular project to learn one! Do not forget the following.

- Projects already running. Unless your IT systems are completely static you may have some projects already running which are using the resource you require for this project. You need to be ruthless in grabbing the resource you require – this is where you may need your top management.
- If you do not have sufficient in-house staff for the project, you need to use the ones you do have wisely. In this project, knowledge of your business, experience of the way IT

works in your organization, and familiarity with the users are most important. Use your in-house staff where you can maximize these assets.
- If your IT is mostly, or completely, outsourced you will need to ensure that your outsourcing company can commit to the timescales you need. This may prove tricky if it does not see its part in this project as part of its contract – advice on how to deal with this is given in Chapter 9.
- Be very careful about dependencies between tasks. Where systems interface, and where they run under the control of another, and everywhere where you are having to upgrade your hardware and operating systems, you cannot complete your testing until the whole environment is compliant. More of this below, but you need to consider it when you are planning, or you may find that some of your tasks are not possible.

Consultancy and Software Tools

During your planning stage you may well find that you need help! This may be before or even after you start investigating the compliance of your inventory – and there are plenty of organizations ready to offer their help to you. As soon as the Millennium problem began to be noticed, advertisements could be found in the computer press for consultancy firms and software tools. In fact, some people may have found out about the problem by reading advertisements offering to help them with it!

You may have no choice but to look for help – but you need to consider very carefully what sort of help you require, as much now commands a very high price, and the price is getting higher as we approach the Millennium. You need to consider whether you need advice, tools to automate your processes, or bodies. In more detail the sort of help you can obtain falls broadly into three categories (although many organizations are offering a mixture of two or three of these).

Advice/Consultancy

You can commission consultancy firms to do a complete audit of the Millennium compliance of your organization, produce your inventory for you and record the results of the investigation. Some will even produce the project plan for you, manage the project for you and engage the relevant technical staff to do the program changes. Obviously you can pick which services you require, although some of these firms are now completely booked and will take no further work. Before you choose to sign up for such services you need to remember that you cannot just hand over the project and expect it to happen! You will need to put in a large amount of your knowledge or that of your staff and users, and will need to be available at all times to make decisions. You will also have to ensure that the consultants are committed to meeting your deadlines – even if your contract with them contains heavy non-delivery penalties, this will be little consolation if your organization does not survive the Millennium. This is not to say that such consultancies are inept, or that putting your project into their hands is inherently more risky than doing it yourself, but whenever you involve third parties you need to ensure that everyone understands the project and its goals. Such consultancies are probably not needed if you have strong in-house or outsourced resource unless that resource is engaged on other projects that you cannot put on hold. (In this situation, of course, you might consider bringing in contractors to complete those projects, so that you can use your experienced staff on the Millennium work.) See in this context the section on Solution Provider Agreements in Chapter 9.

THE TECHNICAL ISSUES

Software Tools

There are now plenty of tools available to help you automate both the investigation into the compliance of your programs, and to automate the changes in code necessary to make them compliant. These started in the mainframe environment where typically there are many thousand lines of code to be considered. However, there are now tools available for programs running on mid-range and personal computers. (Many consultancies use these as part of their work). Once again, you need to think carefully about how you will use them before you make your decision. These tools work by identifying dates and listing the lines of code containing them – they can also change the date formats based on parameters you set up.

These programs, however, depend on being able to identify the date in the first place. Some look for items of data with the word 'date' or 'dat' or 'dte' in the description, or look for a particular format of data, such as xx/xx/xx, and may allow you to input the descriptions you want the tool to look for. But unless the programs are coded strictly to standard, a wayward programmer might well have called a date 'Fred' for a joke, or used an individual format, or used the data storage for another reason. (There is a story, which may be apocryphal, of a software house that ordered all its programmers to use four character years, but did not tell them why. Some programmers, short of data storage, used the first two characters of the year for other data, regarding it as superfluous space. Not only were the programs therefore not compliant, but the automated code checkers would have fallen foul of this sort of programming).

Thus these automated tools require much up-front work to set them up, and you may still feel that you need to check for any exceptions. Similarly the tools which can 'fix' programs need to be told how you want the programs fixed – for example you may wish to tell them to replace all two character years with four characters. But you may well need to check their results. You may also feel that such automated coding needs far more testing – and don't forget that you might need to purchase extra hardware to run these tools.

As in the case of consultancy, you may have no choice but to use these programs. However, they can be as expensive as taking on extra resource, and may need just as much, if not more, supervision to ensure that they work correctly. If, however, you have vast amounts of code, or little in-house resource experienced in the code you are wishing to change, they may be an option. (Don't forget, however, that for these, just as for the 'human' resource, you need the program source code in order to be able to investigate).

Contract Resource

If you have some in-house resource, but have identified a shortfall, using contract resource as extra bodies is possibly your best option. This approach has the benefit of flexibility – you can use this resource as you want as long as the contractors have the relevant skills, you can direct it as you please and ensure that the contractors work in the way you want them to. You need to ensure that you draw up a tight contract to be confident that the contractors will stay for as long as you require them and, like everything else, rates are going up. But as long as you have sufficient in-house management and experience, contract staff can be a very useful asset, especially as you can use them for the day to day code investigation and correction, leaving the more 'exciting' investigative work to your in-house staff.

Change Management

Once you have made your plans, and decided how you are going to resource your projects, then the advice given in Chapter 6 applies just as much as right at the beginning of

THE TECHNICAL ISSUES

the project. You need to check your progress against your timeline very carefully, every week. You need to be flexible enough to react to unforeseen circumstances, and you cannot allow anything to slip. There is also another issue that you must not forget at this stage – and this is change management.

Even if you have shelved any other project work, there are always essential changes that need to be made, because of problems and faults, breakdowns of kit and equipment, changes because of new legislation, etc. Because of this you must ensure that you keep change management very carefully under control. In Chapter 4 which dealt with inventories, it was stressed that someone, or some group of people, must 'own' the inventory, and here is where that becomes critical. You need to ensure that any changes are recorded on the inventory, not forgetting the following.

Change of Use

If a PC or embedded chip equipment is passed from one user to another it may become more or less critical to the business, its lifespan may change, it may have something new loaded onto it. All this must be recorded and your plans changed accordingly.

New Equipment

You are almost bound to buy new equipment in the lifespan of this project. Although you would not intentionally buy anything that is not compliant you must be confident that it is and record it anyway. Your inventory needs to reflect all your equipment, not just that required for this project, as the inventory will be crucial to you after the Year 2000. On top of this the new equipment may interface into something already on your plan and you need to record that also.

Program Changes

It is likely that you will have put a freeze on all but essential program changes during the life of the project, but problems will arise. Your inventory is unlikely to record each program of a system – but an individual program may need changing to fix a problem at the same time that it is being changed to make it compliant. You will need to decide how you deal with this problem – you cannot copy into production a program which has not been completely finished, yet you must reflect the change in the Millennium compliant version. Typically programmers take a copy of a production program, change it to make it compliant, and then copy it into production again. You need to ensure that you do not 'lose' any changes during this process. Most established IT teams have change management processes in place to deal with this. If, however, you have employed consultants to change your programs, they may have taken a copy of the system off site to change it. When it is returned to you for implementation, you need to ensure that any changes to the programs done by you are reflected in the system delivered by the consultants.

Testing

You may think that this is in the wrong chapter, but you need to consider how you are going to test your systems when you are planning your project. Clearly you need to test your systems as thoroughly as possible but how do you go about this? This is an extremely difficult issue, and not one to which there is necessarily any real answer. Here, however, are a few issues for you to think about.

- If you have 'repaired' or amended systems, your first tests need to establish that they still work in 1998 and 1999. Although this sounds self-evident, it is unlikely

THE TECHNICAL ISSUES

that you will decide to implement all your new and changed systems as a 'big bang' on the evening of 31st December, 1999! You must, therefore, ensure that your Millennium changes have not affected the successful running of the code before 2000. You need to plan for time to test this first. Once you have established this, you can start using your systems now – but do not forget that you have not tested them thoroughly for the Millennium.

- Most application systems can be tested by feeding into them data which contains dates in the Year 2000. Programmers will normally do this as part of their first or 'unit' tests, and this does establish that the program has been changed correctly. The next step is to test the programs all running together as a system, and again you can create special data to test this.

The last step, however, is the most difficult. Even system testing a suite of programs does not really prove that the system will work successfully in the Year 2000 – it simply tests that those programs will run successfully. To be absolutely sure you need to run the system on Millennium compliant hardware and operating system, and on hardware that thinks that it is the Year 2000. How can you do this?

- If you are lucky enough to have spare kit, or if you hold backup equipment for disaster recovery, you could set the date on this equipment to a date in the Year 2000 and then test all the other software on it. This is the safest way to proceed, and if you have the use of this kit for some time, then this provides the best test of all.
- If you have a contract for disaster recovery with a company that supplies replacement kit, you may be able to do a deal with them to supply you with kit to use for this purpose. Some companies are offering testing facilities to which you can take your systems for testing.

- If neither of the above applies then you have more of a problem. You need to try to find times when you can set the dates on your hardware to the Year 2000, but take care! As discussed in Chapter 6, this is a dangerous thing to do and you need to be sure that you will be able to recover the equipment after the test. If you are at all unsure you must check at the very least with the supplier of your backup and restore software that it will work, and you must ensure that you have a clean backup of your entire system, to use in the event of an emergency.
- There are some tools available that will 'spoof' the date – ie supply the operating system with any date you wish. These are mainly in the mainframe environment, and are very useful, but you need to realize that it is not really a full test – your hardware is still running in the current year.

You need to plan, therefore, for all this testing, and make sure you allow enough time for retesting when faults are found. Typically testing can be over 60 per cent of any project, so do not underestimate it. *Do* not forget as well that you need to test for a variety of dates – it is wise to agree an approach for each system – critical dates might be:
- 1st January, 1999 – for any systems you think may sort by year and for backup/archive systems which may assume that the datafield year = '99' is an expiry date
- 1st April, 1999 for financial systems
- 9th September, 1999 for backup/archive systems (possible, but 01/01/1999 is more likely)
- 1st January, 2000 for everything
- 29th February, 2000 for everything and
- 1st March, 2000 (just to make sure)
- 1st April, 2000 – to ensure financial systems can process financial year 00/01
- 1st January, 2001 – to ensure that the coders have not concentrated too much on the Year 2000!

The Ongoing Project

Get on with it!

Once your project has started, you obviously need to continue your planning and managing but, apart from the critical need to ensure that milestone dates do not slip, it is much like every other IT project. Here is some general advice which should prove useful.

- Even if it is not your usual custom, celebrate completion of systems and successful implementations. This project can be a tedious one as staff working on it do not see any staggering benefits. Your staff members are very important so keep their spirits up by praising jobs well done. Consider a logo for the project to give it a real identity, and hold meetings for all staff involved in it.
- Do not exacerbate your problems by buying anything else that is not compliant. Ask the question specifically of everything you purchase from now on and secure appropriate legal warranties where possible. In this context, see the discussion of express and implied warranties in Chapter 9.
- Similarly, ensure that you have statements in all your contracts for supplies and services. You are perfectly within your rights to ask about the Year 2000 projects

THE TECHNICAL ISSUES

your proposed contractors may be running, and if they do not want to tell you – fear the worst.
- Keep up awareness sessions for your staff – and consider them for your customers to circumvent any fears that they may have.
- Think about staff cover over the 1999/2000 Christmas/New Year holiday. You may unusually need more staff rather than less, and if you may have to refuse requests for leave, you need to warn staff now. Remember you may not have a working telephone/paging system, you might not even have lights, so plan your staff cover for the worst eventuality. You can always throw a party if nothing untoward happens!
- Consider implementing corporate standards now, such as always writing the year as 1998 rather than 98 – a small point but it will get the message across.
- And lastly… keep your eye on the ball, try not to panic, and keep others calm. This project is big, critical and risky, but the worst thing you can do is panic. Consider the question 'How do you eat an elephant?' – the answer is 'One bite at a time'. The same goes for this project – you simply have to get on with it, and start as soon as you can!

PART two
THE LEGAL ISSUES

Contract Law

Defining relationships – Which of your business relationships are going to be affected by the Millennium Bug?

INTRODUCTION

As this book demonstrates, many legal issues are raised by the Year 2000. From a business perspective, the focal issue will be liability. There will be considerable legal analysis of who is responsible for preventing or curing Year 2000-related problems. Whilst tortious liability centring around the concept of negligence may well be relevant as discussed later in this book, the contracts dealing with the provision of software, computers and machinery containing embedded chips will be the main battle ground for lawyers.

In nearly all contractual situations, the parties' interests are in conflict. The most basic example is probably price. The higher the price the better for the supplier, the worse for the purchaser. Rather than point out the obvious conflict in each case and draw out how the interests of each party are best served in relation to each issue, we have considered matters predominantly from the user's point of view but would impress upon readers who are suppliers that their legal interests might often be best served by following the opposite course of action. For example, suppliers should endeavour to avoid giving the sorts of warranty suggested in this chapter unless they are completely confident that can meet them in all respects.

In this chapter, we will begin by outlining the case for users to perform a contractual audit before the Year 2000, we will then consider the key types of contractual relationships most likely to be affected by the Year 2000; examining both the legal nature of each relationship and certain Year 2000 issues arising from those relationships. In Chapter 10, we will set out some of the principles and areas of law which may well prove crucial in determining the outcome of Year 2000 disputes based on contractual issues before concluding our review of matters contractual in Chapter 11 which is dedicated to contractual remedies which may be relevant to Year 2000 disputes.

THE CASE FOR A CONTRACTUAL AUDIT

Many users are only now coming to terms with the potential technical ramifications of Year 2000 on their businesses. They have, for the most part, not even contemplated the legal implications. However, it is not only short-sighted but also poor risk management to focus on the technical issues alone at this stage. In the Year 2000 context, the contracts which are typically relevant are those under which the user has received software, hardware, equipment containing embedded chips or services related to any of those. Additionally, any contract covering the supply of goods or services by or to you should be analyzed. Obviously, if resources do not permit, the principle of prioritisation will mean that your greatest focus should be on those contracts affecting key areas of your operation.

The sooner you undertake this analysis the better. The principal reason for addressing the legal situation now rather than later is that the closer we get to the Year 2000, the lower the chances of being able to remedy any problems which you discover.

In the course of this chapter, we will see some of the types of Year 2000 contractual exposure which a comprehensive legal audit may uncover. Much of this exposure will stem from the absence of contractual obligation on your goods and services providers to ensure that your business is unaffected by the Year 2000.

If you discover such a situation sufficiently early you may be able to persuade the relevant supplier to renegotiate the contract to eliminate your areas of concern and, failing this, you may still be able to find an alternative supplier willing to step into the breach.

BI-PARTITE ANALYSIS (OLD AND NEW AGREEMENTS)

Very few contracts entered into prior to, say, 1997 expressly dealt with the Year 2000 and the respective responsibilities of the parties in relation thereto. It is therefore necessary to a certain degree to perform a bi-partite analysis, separating contracts which make no express reference to Year 2000 from those which do. We would hope that once they have read this book, users will ensure that very few, if any, contracts into which they enter will fail to address the Year 2000.

We will see that in the case of existing agreements which are silent in relation to Year 2000, analysis of the relevant provisions may well prove disconcerting for users for various reasons. Contractual provisions cannot be changed unilaterally by a user, and a supplier is unlikely to want to make changes to a contract which are disadvantageous to it. Thus, the options open to a user will typically be to leave things as they are or to carry out a damage limitation exercize which may involve taking various steps such as the termination of unfavourable contracts.

In the case of new contracts, the sort of Year 2000 provisions which should be inserted will be dealt with in the course of this chapter.

IDENTIFYING THE CONTRACTUAL RELATIONSHIPS AFFECTED BY YEAR 2000

Software Licences

Legal Nature

Under the law of England and Wales, copyright in a piece of work vests in the original author of that work unless either the author is an employee, in which case the copyright will vest in the employer or the author assigns copyright to another party.

The owner of copyright is exclusively entitled to perform specific acts in relation to the work. These include the right to copy the work or a substantial part thereof. When using a computer program, a user will need to load it on to its hardware system. This very act of loading involves the creation of a copy of the work and therefore, if carried out by a user without the copyright owner's permission would constitute an infringement of the owner's copyright.

In order to authorize use of a program by a third party, the copyright owner must grant a licence to that user. In granting such a licence, the copyright owner becomes a 'licensor' and the user a 'licensee'. Licences are essentially permissive; granting rights to a person who had no previous rights. The terms of that licence will govern the extent of the permitted use of the software program by the user. It is a loose but common use of terminology to refer to the acquirer of software which is subject to a licence as a 'purchaser'. More precisely, he is a 'licensee'.

It should be pointed out that it need not necessarily be the copyright owner who grants a licence of the software. The copyright owner may have authorized a third party such as a distributor to do so. As with all contracts of supply, it is desirable for the potential customer, in this case the licensee, to take any appropriate steps to confirm that the entity granting the licence is entitled to do so. If the potential licensor is the software house which wrote the program, this is unlikely to be an issue.

Is there an Effective Licence?

Before we further our analysis of the law pertaining to licences in the context of Year 2000, we consider it worthwhile to point out to readers that licences which they consider themselves to have entered into either as users or suppliers may be ineffective. Obviously, if this is the case, the purport of the individual clauses of such licences will be irrelevant. In this connection, we will consider briefly three causes of possible invalidity of apparently valid licences.

Battle of the Forms
If, in the phase of contractual negotiations, the potential licensee does not merely sign on the dotted line of the supplier's licence but instead sends its own purchase order, it may be arguable, depending on the exact circumstances, that the terms of the purchase order rather than the terms of the licence govern the supply of the software. Many contractual cases revolve around the issue of which parties' terms prevail and the result is often that at least one of the parties is surprized that certain terms and conditions on which it considered itself to be dealing do not form part of the contract.

THE LEGAL ISSUES

Privity of Contract

In order to be able to sue or to be sued under a contract, one must be a party to that contract. For example if a father contracts to buy a bicycle for his son and the bicycle proves defective, only the father, not the son can sue the bicycle shop for any available contractual remedies.

In the context of software licences, this legal doctrine becomes particularly relevant when one is considering the legally vexed issue of shrink-wrap licences. The difficulty stems from the fact that the entity from which the user acquires the software is often not the software house named in the shrink-wrap licence. Thus, it is arguable that the contract is between the retailer and its customer and that the terms of the shrink-wrap licence do not form part of the contract. Despite foreign judgements recognising the legal effect of shrink-wrap licences, the validity of such licences remains doubtful in this country.

Non-incorporation

It is a fundamental precept of contract law that for terms of business to be effective, they must be brought to the attention of the potential licensee before the contract is concluded.

A simple example of this principle is encapsulated in the two different disclaimer models adopted by hotel cloakrooms. In one case, you may see a sign above the cloakroom specifically stipulating that 'no responsibility is accepted for loss or damage to the articles which you deposit.' In another case, there may be no such sign outside the cloakroom. However, you may find, if you look, that the ticket handed to you by the cloakroom attendant contains a similar disclaimer on its reverse. Whereas the disclaimer will probably be effective in the first example as your attention had been drawn to the exclusion before you deposited your belongings, in the second case it will be ineffective, having been brought to your attention, if at all, only after you had deposited your valuables.

In the context of software licences, terms which the licensor intends to bind the licensee may not do so. Such terms may be ineffective if contained in invoices or other documentation despatched to the user after it has already committed itself to acquiring the software.

Indeed, this doctrine also casts doubt upon the validity of shrink-wrap licences which, depending on method of sale and packaging, may only come to the acquirer's attention after the 'sale' has already been concluded.

Duration

Software licences are of either fixed or unspecified duration. If in a particular case, the licence in question is of fixed duration and expires before the Millennium change, then, irrespective of the other terms of the licence, the user will not have a case against the software house for the consequences of the failure of the software to handle the Millennium change.

The same may be true in respect of a periodic licence which may lapse if the licensee does not pay the renewal fee at the contractually specified time. For example, if a licence is expressed to be subject to the payment of an annual licence fee and this is payable, say, by 17th December each year, then if the licensee fails to pay the renewal fee by 17th December 1999, the licence may lapse on that date and any obligations of the licensor in respect of Year 2000 compliance could be extinguished.

Matters may be complicated by the combination in one agreement of the grant of a licence and the provision of maintenance services. In such circumstances, if the licensor is on the hook to make the software Year 2000 compliant and the licensee does not want to let the licensor off that hook, it should ensure that it pays all fees due under the agreement whether or not it is clear that they are licence fees, maintenance fees or a combination of both.

The impact of the date of grant of a licence and its duration on the issue of implied warranties and the potential liability of a licensor will be considered in some detail in Chapter 10.

Termination

If the licence is terminable at the option of the licensor for breach of the contract by the licensee for non-payment or other reasons, then the licensee must take care not to breach the contract and thereby give the licensor an easy escape route from any Year 2000 compliance obligations it might have.

Object Code, Source Code and Escrow

Without being excessively technical, there are two languages in which any software program exists. The first, 'object code' can be read by a computer but not by a human being. The supply of programs in object code enables the supplier to give the user as little information as possible about the details of the program, thereby reducing the danger of copying. For this and other reasons, the vast majority of software licences are granted in 'object code'.

Software is occasionally also licensed in 'source code' version. The source code is the human-readable form of the software. Granting access to source code to licensees is resisted strongly by most licensors. The reasons for this reluctance include the fact that loss of exclusive control of the source code by the licensor greatly increases the risk of third parties copying part or all of the program and this, of course, jeopardizes the principal asset of the software house.

However, source code is not only relevant to licensors. In order to maintain or modify a program, access to the source code is generally necessary. In the context of Year 2000, access to the source code could be particularly vital as, if the supplier or maintainer of a software product is unable or unwilling to make the software Year 2000 compliant, a third party with access to the source code might be able to do so. In this context, a half way house, called escrow, exists. Source code escrow agreements allow licensees access to the source code but only in very limited circumstances. Traditionally, these circumstances have been limited to the liquidation of the source code owner or failure by that entity to maintain the software. To take account of the Year 2000, the principal escrow agent in the UK, the National Computing Centre, has recently introduced a third trigger for source code release to licensees, namely the failure of software to be Year 2000 compliant. As with the other source code triggers, the source code owner must be agreeable to such a provision being included in the escrow agreement.

Suffice it to say that any entity becoming a licensee of the object code version of a software program would be well advised to seek to become a beneficiary of such an escrow arrangement. Whether this is possible will depend on various factors.

In general, the higher the licence fee payable, the more likely the software house is to be willing to place the source code in escrow.

The Legal Nature of Software – Goods or Services?

It is appropriate to mention at this juncture one of the most debated legal topics in the context of software. The legal nature of software has not been definitively determined. In brief, the discussion centres on whether for legal purposes, a software program should be considered goods or services. This is relevant to various legal issues. These include the nature of the warranties implied into a contract for the provision of software and the ability of the supplier contractually to exclude such terms. This debate and its potential effects in the context of Year 2000 will be dealt with at length in Chapter 10.

Express and Implied Warranties

In the Year 2000 technical audit that most IT users will or at least should have performed, the central issue will be to establish which parts of their commercial infrastructure would be adversely affected by the Year 2000 if they were not to take appropriate remedial action. One of the elements in this audit is to find out from the supplier whether what it has supplied or will supply to the user is or will be made Year 2000 compliant.

In this context, we must return to the concept of the bi-partite analysis discussed in Chapter 9 above in relation to the case for a contractual audit.

Several forests of questionnaires have already been issued by users to suppliers trying to ascertain just this (see Appendix B). There are also databases comprising such information in relation to various different products. One of the best known of these is located on the Internet at *www.weblaw.co.uk.* In the main, questionnaires and databases are only really relevant to fact finding missions by existing users of products who wish to determine the capacity of those products to deal with the Year 2000. As the contracts governing the use of such products are already in place, there may be little if anything that a user can do to improve its position.

The situation is quite different for anyone entering into any software licence between now and 2000. They should insist on an express warranty being written into the contract to the effect that the software is totally Year 2000 compliant (see Appendix D). For the avoidance of doubt, this warranty is in addition to and not in substitution for the normal types of express warranties which one would expect in a software licence, such as that the licensor is legally entitled to grant the licence. The existence and wording of such a Year 2000 compliance warranty clause could ultimately prove vital in the determination of whether the user has a case against the licensor in the event that the software proves not to be Year 2000 compliant.

The definition of what constitutes 'Year 2000 compliance' is complicated and vital. Simplistically, one could describe the essence of the issue to be whether the performance or functionality of the software is adversely affected by the Year 2000 or any other date change. The BSI has established a definition which is being adopted by many users and suppliers in this field. This is reproduced in Appendix A.

As in many cases, software suppliers are still working on making their products Year 2000 compliant or intend doing so between now and 2000, one may find oneself obliged to accept a compliance warranty that will only 'kick in' sometime between now and 2000. This is definitely an area where proper legal advice should be sought from a firm with expertize in these matters.

If a user accepts a prospective warranty of this nature, it should keep a keen eye on the clock to determine whether the supplier is on course to carry out such remedial work. In any event, contingency plans should be established to cater for the possibility of non-compliance. An escrow arrangement, as discussed above, providing for source code release to the user in the event that the software has not been made compliant by the supplier by a certain date may be appropriate.

In the event of Year 2000 non-compliance of software and the absence of an express Year 2000 warranty, users may have to fall back on warranties which the law implies into contracts for the protection of users. As indicated above, in the context of software, implied warranties constitute a particularly complicated issue and are therefore dealt with separately in Chapter 10.

Software Development Agreements

If an IT user is unable to find a suitable software package on the general market, it may be necessary for him to commission a software house to develop what it needs. This may involve the software house writing a new program from scratch or customizing one of its existing packages.

In the case of bespoke or customized software, the development work will normally be regulated by the terms of a software development agreement. The nature and extent of the customer's rights in the software once it has been successfully developed, will be a vital issue.

Acceptance tests are a standard feature of agreements where an IT user is not simply becoming a licensee of a product already on the market but commissioning a software developer to create an application customized to its particular requirements. If a user has been well advised, it will often have had a technical and/or functional specification drawn up either in-house or by an independent consultant. Such a specification should stipulate unambiguously that the software must be Year 2000 compliant. Acceptance tests are often based on whether the software developed meets such specifications.

Obviously, the point of the tests is to determine whether the software does what it is supposed to do. Hence, the tests by reference to an appropriately drafted specification or otherwise should expressly include provision for testing the Year 2000 compliance of the software.

Typically, the product once written or customized will be licensed to the user, as set out above. However, the fact that the development or customization costs of a program have been specifically paid for by a particular user will mean that the user may well be able to obtain more than a simple object code licence. At most, it will procure an assignment of the copyright in that software as considered in the section below on software sales.

Short of an assignment, it may be able to obtain a source code licence or become entitled to source code release under an escrow arrangement as described above.

Software Sales

Users should beware that there is a legal rule of general application whereby copyright vests in an entity which is commissioned to develop software or any other work. This means that unless a contract provides to the contrary, the developer, despite having been paid for his work will own the copyright in the software and the user will merely have the right to use that software.

As discussed above, from a legal perspective, the normal method of software supply is by way of licence. However, in certain cases an entity commissioning a software house to write a software program will not want to be subject to the inherently limited form of grant which is a licence but will want to have unrestricted rights to do whatever it wishes with the software including licensing it to third parties or even selling it on. In such a case, the appropriate form of agreement is one of sale, such sale to cover all the intellectual property rights pertaining to the software.

Whether this will be analysed as a sale of goods or a supply of services will be considered in Chapter 10.

Software Maintenance Agreements

Even where a software developer implements state of the art quality control methodology during the software development process, almost every program will contain a considerable number of errors or bugs. Errors may result from the user using the software in a way not anticipated by the developer.

No user can be certain that the software it acquires will be free of such problems. Software licences often contain provisions which stipulate that:

- the software is not error free
- the software is supplied on an 'as is' basis
- the implied condition as to fitness for purpose is excluded (the applicability of implied conditions to software is considered in Chapter 10)
- it is the responsibility of the potential licensee to satisfy itself that the software is fit for the purpose which it has in mind.

Whilst software houses often address and rectify problems in a subsequent release of the software, there is generally no guarantee that they will and that even if they do, that such release will be available soon enough for the user's business. Furthermore, the entitlement to such future releases may be contingent on the licensee having a maintenance agreement in place with the supplier.

Nowadays, when businesses are often highly dependent on the efficient functioning of their IT systems, the user must get errors corrected; those that are serious, immediately. It is true that contractual warranties may provide for rectification of certain problems within a limited period of time. If these are comprehensive warranties, then the maintenance agreement need only 'kick in' when the warranties expire. However, if as is the norm, the warranties do not provide the full range of support services covered by a typical maintenance contract, it usually makes sense for the user to supplement the warranties with a maintenance contract which takes effect at the start of the licence term.

It is vital rather than optional for most business users to have proper maintenance agreements in place in order to be able to procure quick and efficient assistance to rectify software problems that arise. The provision of such maintenance may cover on-site visits as a back-up where telephonic assistance proves unsatisfactory. Such agreements will often categorize different fault levels and oblige the maintainer to meet fixed response and repair times.

Let us now examine the relevance of maintenance agreements in the context of our theme. The fundamental issue is whether the maintainer is obliged to make the software which is subject to the agreement Year 2000 compliant. Obviously, this is only relevant if the software is not compliant and the licensor is not going to make it so under the licence agreement.

Limitation periods are an additional factor to be considered. As is pointed out in Chapter 17, an entity which wishes to sue on the basis of a contractual breach has six years in which to institute proceedings. In the case of the supply of software, this period will probably be measured as from the date of supply of the software. Thus, a software user who acquired a product under licence in 1993 may discover that for Year 2000 purposes it is already out of time before it finds the non-compliance.

In Chapters 12 and 17 which deal with tort and dispute resolution respectively, we consider the alternative route of suing in tort for negligence. However, contractual claims are to be favoured where available as, amongst other things, they may well result in higher awards of damages.

If a user gets to Year 2000 and finds itself out of time to launch a contractual claim based on the licence, it may discover that it is still in a position to sue the maintainer in contract on the basis of a breach of the maintenance obligations. The reason for this is quite simple. Maintenance contracts are generally annually renewable. Thus, if a maintainer was explicitly or implicitly obliged under the terms of a maintenance contract in force in Year 2000 to make a software product Year 2000 compliant, the customer would have until some time in 2006 to sue.

In this connection, it is relevant to note that the maintainer and the licensor are often one and the same. Thus, although a claim based on a maintenance contract would differ from one based on a licence, one would, in essence, have two bites at the same cherry.

However, to some extent, one must look at these issues in isolation as while a licensor under the terms of the licence may not be responsible for making the software compliant, it may be liable to do so under the terms of the maintenance agreement. The reverse may also apply.

Old and New Agreements

In this context, it is again useful to perform a bi-partite analysis; dividing maintenance contracts which make no express reference to Year 2000 from the vast minority, namely those that do.

Old Agreements
Agreements already in place will typically make no reference to Year 2000. The question will therefore be whether the general responsibilities of the maintainer under a particular contract would be interpreted by a court as extending to an obligation to make the software in question compliant.

The law implies an obligation on maintenance providers to perform their functions with 'reasonable care and skill'. This is not likely to be of enormous assistance.

The obligations of a maintenance provider vary from contract to contract. It may be the case that the maintainer will not have taken on any obligations in relation to the user's software other than to keep it operating in accordance with the user documentation provided by the supplier. However, almost invariably, there is some responsibility on the maintainer to correct defects or errors in the software. It is likely that in many cases this will be construed as a basis for holding the maintainer liable for making the software Year 2000 compliant.

A peculiar feature of Year 2000 is that it will create problems in software which has run perfectly well for many years. As the user may well find itself in the strange position of being aware that something will go wrong with the software well in advance of its actually doing so, must it sit and wait for such problems to arise or can it oblige its service provider to act on a preventative basis? Typically, agreements will not provide for such preventative maintenance. In the exceptional case where one does, analysis of the particular terms of the agreement will be necessary to determine whether Year 2000 non-compliance problems would be covered.

New Agreements
If we turn now to new contracts, ie those which have yet to be entered into or which may be amended on renewal prior to Year 2000, the scenario can be very different. The ideal from the user's point of view is to have the maintainer agree expressly in the terms of the contract that it is its exclusive responsibility whether as part of its error correction, update or other duties to make the software in question compliant well before the Year 2000. This should be an integral part of the maintenance service for which no extra fee is payable. If a user can get a statement such as this in a contract, then subject to the maintainer going bust or finding an escape hatch from the contract, the user should have him 'bang to rights' in the event of the software failing or faltering on account of non-compliance.

A user may be able to have a contract which is silent on this point amended to cover it by virtue of agreement with the maintainer at the time the contract comes up for renewal.

Obviously, if a maintainer analyses its own potential exposure in relation to Year 2000 and concludes that it may be on the hook to make software compliant, it may also form the view that this is an obligation that it would rather avoid. Hence it is crucial on the part of the user to ensure to the extent possible that the contract does not facilitate such escapology.

In this context, one of the types of clause of which a user should be wary is one which gives the maintainer a right to terminate the contract on, say, six months' notice. A user does not want to receive such notice in or shortly before June 1999. Indeed, with regard to contractual audits, it may be this kind of clause which rings the loudest alarm bells.

Finally, we should add that in many cases the software in question may be completely compliant or the licensor may have undertaken to make it so well in advance of the Year 2000. In such cases, whatever the contractual provisions, the Year 2000 should not result in extra work for the maintainer.

However, from the user's point of view, it is not necessarily sufficient to rely on the word of the software provider and, for good measure, the maintainer should be obliged at the very least to carry out some testing on the software to verify its Year 2000 compliance.

Thus, if the software is licensed to a user by one party but maintained by another, the user would be well advised to insist on appropriate express warranties from both the licensor and the maintainer of the type described above.

If the intellectual property rights in the software are owned by you by virtue of an assignment from the developer, you may have obtained a Year 2000 compliance warranty and indemnity in the assignment. However, even in such circumstances, you should be intent on obtaining a Year 2000 warranty from the maintainer.

Hardware Procurement

Unfortunately, non-compliance is not a problem limited to software. It affects computers and a vast amount of the machinery which incorporates embedded chips. No reliable statistics are available for the number of computers affected by the Year 2000 syndrome but there is little doubt that it would be alarmingly high. Indeed, at the time of writing, a class action has been started in the USA against five leading PC manufacturers on account of the non-compliance of computers which they have sold.

Before we address the legal issues, let us briefly consider the technical nature of the problem, which is dealt with in more detail in the technical part of this book (Chapters 1–8).

Certainly, the majority of people buying a PC in 1998 would, if they considered the issue at all, assume it to be completely Year 2000 compliant. Unfortunately, this is not the case.

If one were to describe the non-compliance of computers and software as a nightmare, then the situation *vis-à-vis* embedded chips could, without hyperbole, be said to be a potential catastrophe. At least with software there is a known solution that can be effected, however expensive and time-consuming that may prove and with hardware the existence of the problem can be determined.

With embedded chips, the problem is far more insidious. Every piece of equipment, containing an embedded chip, whether it be a lift, a blood transfusion machine or an aircraft control device, is susceptible to the same non-compliance problem. The consequences of non-compliance and resultant equipment failure have been the focus of much recent media attention; at worst they could be fatal.

In many cases the user of the equipment will not even realize that there is an embedded chip in the piece of machinery that it is using and even those who are aware may not know how to access let alone test the Year 2000 compliance of that chip.

The problem is compounded by the meandering intricacy of many supply chains, which will mean that even if one raises the issue with the equipment supplier, it will often not know how to deal with chips or even be aware of who encoded them. As if that were not bad enough, Taskforce 2000 reported last year that in the case of two seemingly identical pieces of equipment from the same batch, one may be compliant and one not.

Hopefully, the reader will see from this overview of the problem that the legal audit of the existing IT related agreements should not be limited to software and computers but should additionally cover every significant item of machinery which forms part of the operation. Indeed, as there may effectively be no technical solution with such machinery, the legal position will be all the more important.

Old and New Agreements

Again, in this context, it is helpful to enter into a bi-partite analysis of the legal situation, separating those contracts already entered into and which are silent on the Year 2000 issue from those yet to be entered, where it is to be hoped that specific Year 2000 compliance provisions can be incorporated.

Old Agreements

There is probably little comfort that can be offered to users who have already entered into computer purchase or other hardware procurement contracts not containing any such express Year 2000 provisions. The resolution of any disputes in relation to such systems will probably revolve around the question of whether the warranties implied by law into such contracts have been breached by the supply of non-compliant systems. These implied warranties, which are considered in Chapter 10, particularly in the context of their possible application to software, are the implied warranties of satisfactory quality and fitness for purpose. In determining whether these implied warranties cover Year 2000 compliance of products sold, the date of supply of the products is bound to play a role. In brief and somewhat simplistically, the greater the interval between the time of supply and the Year 2000, the less likely it is that those warranties will be construed as covering Year 2000 compliance.

Whilst we are focusing on contracts for the sale of goods, it should not be forgotten that much hardware is provided under leasing contracts. The fundamental difference between these two types of contract is that ownership of the goods does not pass to the customer under the leasing model. The customer's entitlement is limited to possession and use of the goods during a fixed or variable period of time, although such agreements often contain an option to purchase, which, if exercized, leads into a separate contract of sale.

Whilst there are obviously fundamental differences between the legal and commercial nature of contracts of sale and lease, the warranties implied into both categories of contracts for the protection of the customer are the same, namely satisfactory quality and fitness for the purpose for which the items were supplied.

Of course, in the case of leasing contracts, the customer may have escape routes if it suspects non-compliance, either by way of termination or a right to a replacement item. Obviously, this will depend on the terms of the contract.

New Agreements
As regards contracts for the procurement of computers and equipment that the reader enters into between now and Year 2000, it should as with software contracts, endeavour to negotiate into the contract an appropriate Year 2000 compliance warranty. A model of such a warranty is given in Appendix D. Of course, the chances of a consumer buying a single PC from a computer retailer managing to alter the terms of the sale contract are infinitesimal. A large corporate buying several thousand might be somewhat more successful.

Where the prospective purchaser is unsure whether the new item of equipment which it wishes to purchase contains embedded chips, it should adopt a line of caution and assume that it does and therefore endeavour to obtain an appropriate compliance warranty.

Hardware Maintenance Contracts

Whereas software maintenance is most often obtained from the software supplier itself, hardware support is often procured from a third party which specializes in providing maintenance for equipment provided by different manufacturers to a single user. These companies may be completely independent or have a contract with a computer manufacturer to provide maintenance for its customers. On purchasing a computer, there are often tied maintenance contracts which are available from the supplier.

From the user's point of view, a third party maintainer may make the IT user's job far simpler because it will give it a single port of call for any hardware support it requires. This is particularly desirable if, as is often the case, different hardware elements, such as printers, computers and cabling have been obtained from three different suppliers.

One advantage of having a maintenance contract with the supplier of the equipment rather than a third party is that the user avoids the potential consequences of poor relationships between the supplier and a third party maintainer. For example, the supplier may, amongst other matters, make it difficult for the third party maintainer to obtain spare parts. Without considering the legality of such a refusal, it is clear that this could create practical problems for a user who is dependent on such a third party.

As with software maintenance contracts, an express provision whereby the maintainer agrees to make the subject-matter of the contract Year 2000 compliant is the ideal from the user's perspective. The value of the implied warranty that the maintainer will use its 'reasonable care and skill' is dubious.

Facilities Management/Outsourcing

There is an ever increasing trend for IT users to use the services of third parties, namely facilities managers and outsourcers to manage their IT infrastructure.

It is important at the outset to specify what is meant by the terms 'facilities manager' and 'outsourcer'. The terms are often used interchangeably. Strictly speaking, we consider this to be inaccurate. The normal role of a facilities manager is to take over the in-house systems of an IT user and run them on behalf of that user, typically at the user's offices. Additionally, it may well take on some or all of the user's staff. An outsourcer on the other hand will not adopt the systems previously run by the user in-house. It will run its own systems, typically from its own offices and without recruiting any of the user's personnel. Many users turn to outsourcing for financial reasons and one of the most important factors in that equation is that they will no longer have to bear the cost of maintaining the necessary systems and staff.

From a legal perspective, the distinction between facilities managers and outsourcers is very important. Whereas a facilities manager, like a maintenance company, is dealing with software belonging to the user, the outsourcer is not.

Before we examine the two categories of service separately, we would offer a few words of caution which apply to both and to some extent to any contract governing the provision of services. Besides the two categories of service dealt with here, we would, in particular, refer the reader in this context to maintenance contracts.

The basic approach to adopt when negotiating contracts with service providers is to take nothing for granted. Whatever the exact nature of the service which the user requires, it must ensure that the contract makes express and unequivocal provision to the effect that the service levels must be unaffected by the Millennium change. Moreover, there must be no pre-Year 2000 escape hatch for the service provider. In each case, with the possible exceptions of user non-payment or user liquidation, there should be no provision allowing the service provider to terminate the contract prior to the Millennium change

Facilities Management Contracts

Typically, the facilities manager's obligations in respect of third party software will only cover usage of that software on behalf of the user and liaison with licensors and maintainers of that software. The liaison function should be expressly stated to include timely invocation of any licence warranties or maintenance obligations which relate to making the software in question Year 2000 compliant. However, if there are no such provisions in place, the onus to make the managed systems Year 2000 compliant would be likely to fall on the user, and not the facilities manager.

Where the facilities manager's duties extend to procurement and negotiation of software development, software licence and maintenance contracts on behalf of the user, the contract should clearly oblige the facilities manager to procure appropriate Year 2000 protection for the user, including express warranties, acceptance testing provisions and source code escrow arrangements as detailed above.

If the facilities manager's functions also encompass writing software on behalf of the user or licensing its own software to the user, the manager's position in respect of such software is analogous to that of a software supplier and the observations made above in relation to a software development agreement or licence will apply.

Outsourcing Agreements

The position with outsourcers is different. Their obligations are usually expressed in terms of service levels. Practically, this means that the outsourcer is obliged to produce certain results in specified time frames throughout the course of the contract. It should be no excuse for an outsourcer to say in the Year 2000 aftermath that it was unable to produce those results because the systems on which it relied were not wholly Year 2000 compliant.

An outsourcer which fails to meet service levels on account of its systems' inability to deal with the Millennium change is *prima facie* liable for breach of contract. Isolated breaches may be sanctioned by the award of rebates against the charges for the following period. In the event of repeated or severe failure, the user should be entitled to terminate the agreement and recover some if not all moneys paid under the contract.

It should be made perfectly clear in the contract that these remedies do not preclude any other rights or remedies of the user, such as the right to sue for damages at common law.

In the context of service interruption or, worse, total failure on account of the advent of the Year 2000, damages may be the only remedy which is even vaguely satisfactory.

In view of the facts that the nature of the obligations of an outsourcer are absolute and that if the outsourcer's systems fail, it is likely to breach its contractual obligations to numerous, and possibly all of its customers, it is particularly important for the user to satisfy itself as far as possible, in the pre-contractual phase of the ability of the outsourcer to pay out should it be faced by a barrage of successful claims from its customers post-2000. Appropriate measures will typically include a company search, checking out the outsourcer's insurance position and securing any available parent company guarantees.

Goods and Services Supply Agreements – Supply Chain Management

Few readers will be in any doubt that it is a momentous task in terms of time, effort and money to make one's own company fully Year 2000 compliant. If a company has managed to achieve this, it is not difficult to imagine how the managing director would feel on discovering that his own company's compliance had been undermined by the non-compliance of third parties from which it obtains goods or services.

Hence the fact that BT, which has put enormous effort into getting its own house in order, has written to its 1,800 core suppliers warning them that unless they can show that they are equipped to deal with the Millennium problem, they will no longer be used by the company. The same company has also sounded all sorts of alarm bells about the effect on international traffic if other telecom companies fail to make themselves compliant.

The knock-on effect could be a relatively simply matter of late delivery or failure to deliver by companies whose own stock control and delivery systems are affected by the Millennium Bug. It could also be a more insidious technical affair like the case of the receipt of non-compliant data feeds which throw the recipient company's IT systems into turmoil.

One can request a statement of compliance from one's suppliers. This request should be set out in such a way as to make it totally clear that you are only willing to continue business with your supplier if it satisfies you that it is or will be totally compliant. A model format is included in Appendix C. Many suppliers will not yet be in a position where they can give such an unequivocal statement. Thus, unless alternative suppliers can give you such satisfaction, you may find yourself in a position of having to accept a declaration to the effect that the supplier's operation will be compliant before Year 2000 and seek confirmation closer to the time.

Indeed, one might have cause to be suspicious should an unqualified compliance statement be immediately forthcoming. Unfortunately, once again, the truth of the matter is that whatever your supplier states, the reality may be very different. This does not mean that you should not endeavour to obtain a warranty and representation of compliance as, subject to the solvency point mentioned elsewhere in this book, these may be of significant legal value should your supplier turn out not to be compliant.

Solution Provider Agreements

In an effort to ensure that their IT systems do not fail partially or completely on account of the advent of the Year 2000, IT users are engaging the services of outside software engineers to scrutinize and amend their software programs as necessary.

Whereas all the other contractual relationships identified in this chapter relate to the impact of Year 2000 on pre-existing types of contracts, solution provider contracts have entered existence as a direct consequence of the inability of software to handle the Year 2000 and various other dates. Many IT users have only woken up late to the realization that the problem of IT systems being unable to cope with the Millennium change is not just a theoretical problem which has no direct effect.

It is clear that an enterprize with sufficient time, manpower and money can fix the problem. Whereas for larger companies, the principal problem is the lack of time – by the time you are reading this, less than 600 days will remain – for the average small to medium size enterprize an additional difficulty will be lack of available funds and skills. Many of these smaller entities will find themselves in a 'Catch 22' situation, being unable to raise the funds to fix the problem but risking disaster if they do not.

Although the rates for Year 2000 services are soaring, the necessary skills can still be bought in. However, many of the most established and substantial service providers are so busy that they have already closed their books.

The phenomenal demand has led to numerous companies, doubtlessly of very varying abilities, rushing to offer themselves as Year 2000 solution providers. In the headlong rush for lifeboats, many IT users may find themselves with no option but to engage the services of Year 2000 solution providers, whose track record may be non-existent.

In the despair, users should not forget that it is vital that the solution provider actually commits itself contractually to do what the user needs it to do. There are various methodologies which can be applied and these are considered in the technical part of this book (Chapters 1–8). Obviously, the time for completion of the service must be clearly set out. Ideally, the deadline will be on or before 31 December, 1998 so that the user will have a full year in which to test all its business processes including year-end routines before the Millennium arrives.

Warranties

The user should insist, if at all possible, on a warranty from the solution provider to fix the problem by a certain date. The wording of such a warranty needs to be carefully drafted. A warranty simply stating that 'the solution provider will make the user's software Year 2000 compliant' whilst far preferable from the user's point of view to no warranty is far from ideal. A better *modus operandi* would be to refer to a pre-established standard such as that of the BSI, which is reproduced in Appendix A.

Not every solution provider will get the job totally right and there are bound to be numerous cases of non-compliant software even where solution providers are supposed to have eliminated the problems.

One must also bear in mind the commercial reality that, whilst an appropriately worded warranty may provide legal comfort, it may not be worth the paper it is written on if the warrantor is unlikely to be able to pay out any damages awarded for breach of such warranty. This reinforces the basic point that even if desperate, one should not appoint a solution provider in which one does not have complete faith.

From the solution provider's point of view, an absolute commitment to make the user's systems Year 2000 compliant might prove very onerous and should be avoided if possible.

Another point to bear in mind in what is clearly a seller's market is that solution providing companies are finding it difficult to hold on to their best professionals, who are being lured away by competitors. If you are not convinced that your chosen solution provider has strength in depth in terms of the quality of its consultants, you should endeavour to obtain a warranty to the effect that certain named preferred individuals will carry out your job. Whilst such a warranty does not ensure that the named individuals will remain on your job, it may give the user certain legal rights against the solution provider should it fail to provide such continuity.

From the solution provider's point of view, it should endeavour to ensure that it keeps hold of its best personnel through 'golden handcuffs'. This could be backed up by a keyman insurance policy.

In short, it is essential that the user does not simply sign on the dotted line of the solution provider's terms and conditions. These are unlikely to guarantee anything and may result in the user simply deferring the non-compliance problem to a time when it is far too late to remedy. There are certainly a great number of Year 2000 solution provider contracts in circulation which offer no compliance guarantee whatsoever. This is one of those areas where the understandable impulse of trying to avoid incurring lawyer's fees may prove very counter-productive.

THE LEGAL ISSUES

Exclusion/Limitation of Liability

It is common practice for software suppliers to exclude or, at least, limit their liability for indirect and consequential losses suffered by any users of their products. Such limitations and exclusions may well be very reasonable in the normal commercial context. However, clauses limiting such liability in the context of a Year 2000 solution provider agreement may be far less acceptable as one of the user's principal reasons for engaging the services of the solution provider will typically be the avoidance of such losses.

Contract Law

Relevant principles and issues – How to determine what contractual rights you may have against your suppliers

FRAMEWORK FOR YEAR 2000 CONTRACTUAL ANALYSIS

There is no doubt that many losses will be incurred by many IT users as a result of problems which arise with IT systems and machinery containing embedded chips on account of the date change.

As pointed out elsewhere in this book, from the user's point of view, it is generally preferable to sue on the basis of a contract. If this is not possible, a suit in tort on the basis of the negligence of the supplier may be possible. The analysis of potential actions in tort in the context of Year 2000 is covered in Chapter 12.

We have considered above the sort of contractual relationships most likely to be affected by the Year 2000. However, the fact that the area of a user's business operation which sustains the problems was provided or managed by a third party does not automatically mean that the third party is liable for the losses suffered by the user.

Before any disgruntled user fires off a writ at any supplier, it would be well advised to analyse the contractual position linking it to the supplier to determine whether the user's legal position backs up its feeling of indignation. There are many reasons relating to the contents of or omissions from a contract which may prevent a user who has experienced Year 2000 problems succeeding in an action based on contract against a supplier.

Typically, the last thing a user will want to do is to throw good money after bad by incurring costs in relation to an unsuccessful attempt to obtain assistance or recover damages from that supplier.

With these thoughts in mind, we will proceed to examine some of the legal issues which need to be considered in determining whether the user has an arguable case.

Pre-Contractual Caution

Before the reader becomes involved in the niceties of contract law, we would proffer a few words of pre-contractual pragmatic caution in relation to what are known as entire agreement clauses and the finances of the party with whom you are intending to contract. If this advice is ignored, the rest of the chapter may be of little value to the reader.

Entire Agreement Clauses

One should never rely on the oral assurances of another party to a contract. Nearly all contracts contain what is known as an 'entire agreement clause', which excludes from the ambit of the agreement between the parties all terms which are not expressly written into the contract unless both parties agree to a post-contractual variation of the contract.

Thus, the pre-contractual reassurance from a salesman to the effect that the software was Year 2000 compliant will probably be completely useless to the user unless it was reproduced in the contract itself. If the reader already finds itself in such a position, there may be some mileage in an action for misrepresentation (as considered in Chapter 12 on tort), but this would typically be a fairly desperate, last ditch measure. The doctrine of estoppel which may act to produce exceptions to the entire agreement principle is considered below.

Solvency of Supplier

However well one is advised legally and however comprehensive one's contractual protection, the fact remains that unless the goods or services provider with whom one contracts is financially solvent at the time one wishes to sue it, the best drawn contractual provisions may be completely useless. Therefore, it is always important to assess the financial position of service providers before giving them one's business. In this assessment, their insurance position may be fundamental.

Jurisdiction and Applicable Law

Much trade in the world today is cross-border. In instances where the parties to a contract are based in different jurisdictions, there may be difficulties in establishing in which country and on the basis of which country's law any dispute should be determined.

Thus, it will be far from clear in many cases that a UK based licensee of software who wants to sue a foreign supplier in respect of a product which is not Year 2000 compliant will end up doing so in the UK and on the basis of the laws of England.

Parties to a contract often agree in the contract itself on a choice of law. If they do not, the principle generally applied is that the governing law is that of the country with which the contract is most closely connected.

The matter is further complicated by the fact that in certain circumstances a combination of laws may be applied. This could arise because a court in a particular country is required to adjudge a dispute in relation to a contract which expresses itself to be subject to the laws of another country. Whilst the court may apply the foreign laws generally, on certain issues, possibly including consumer protection, the laws of the country in which the court is situated may apply mandatorily.

The analysis below is based on the laws of England, but readers should be aware that in accordance with what we have said above, this may not be what happens in practice.

Existence of a Contract

It is not always clear whether a contract exists and, if so, on what terms it is based. Two principal elements are as discussed below.

Offer and Acceptance

There are various legal pre-requirements for a contract to come into existence. One of these is that there must be an offer which is accepted. How does this sit with the situation where a supplier sends a potential customer a copy of its terms of business and the customer sends the supplier its purchase order, incorporating its own terms? It is highly unlikely that these two sets of terms do not conflict in certain areas. How one determines whether there is a contract and, if so, which terms regulate it in what is commonly known as the 'battle of the forms' can be quite complicated matters. For example, would there be a contract if a Year 2000 solution provider offered to fix version 5.1 of a software program for a user and the user wrote back and accepted the solution provider's offer to fix version 6.1 of that program? Or, what if the solution provider's offer was stated to be on the basis that the price quoted excluded VAT but the purchase order stated that all prices quoted by suppliers are deemed to include VAT, whether or not they purport to exclude it.

These hypothetical scenarios are intended to serve as examples of the proposition that what appears to be a contract may not be, and that even if there is a contract, its precise terms are not always evident.

Matters may be aggravated where the contractual negotiations were not recorded in writing.

Consideration

A further legal requirement for the coming into existence of a contract is the existence of consideration. Simply stated, this means that each party to a contract must derive a benefit, however strange or small in return for its undertakings in that contract. Let us take the example of a software house that granted a licence to a particular user in 1990 to use a particular product in return for a one-off licence fee. In 1998, the software house receives a questionnaire from that licensee requesting confirmation that the product is Year 2000 compliant. The software house believes the product to be compliant and replies in the affirmative. The product ultimately turns out not to be compliant and the licensee suffers losses. In these circumstances, it is far from clear that a user will succeed in a claim for damages against the software house. The reason is that the software house received no consideration for its compliance statement as the licence fee had already been paid. To avoid such a situation, a licensee would be well advised to provide some consideration, even if nominal to the software house for its confirmation or to have the confirmation given in the form of a deed in respect of which there is no consideration requirement.

Users should also beware of the ability of this doctrine to

operate to their benefit where a service provider requires a supplementary payment for doing something that it is already bound to do contractually.

For example, if an outsourcer demands and receives an extra payment from an existing customer for warranting that its service will not be interrupted by the advent of the Year 2000, the customer might be able to recover that payment if, as is probably the case, the outsourcer was already bound under the terms of the existing contract to provide a continuous service.

IMPLIED TERMS

We referred earlier in this chapter to the contractual phenomenon known as the entire agreement clause. The basic precept is that if a contract contains an entire agreement clause, only provisions expressly included in the contract in its written form will form part of that contract. This precept must be tempered by reference to the existence of terms which are implied into a contract. These fall into various categories which are considered below. The most important in the context of Year 2000 are probably those which are implied as a result of statutory provisions; these include the implied warranties relating to merchantable/satisfactory quality, fitness for purpose and reasonable skill and care.

It should be noted at the outset of this section that terms which would in certain circumstances be implied may in certain cases be excluded by express terms of the contract. This will be considered further along in this chapter under 'Limitation'.

Terms implied by Common Law

We identify below in outline some of the types of term which are liable to be implied by the courts into contracts, where these are likely to be relevant from a Year 2000 perspective.

Software will be fit for the Purpose for which it was Supplied

This could be applied to a software product commissioned by a user and developed through the supply of a combination of goods and services. The right for a licensee of software to correct any inherent defects is only applicable where the software is deemed to constitute goods rather than services, an issue which is considered below in this chapter under 'The Legal Nature of Software'. This could be argued to include fixing Year 2000 non-compliance.

Duration of Contracts of Unspecified Length

In standard works on the law of contract, implied terms relating to the duration of a contract would not merit separate categorization and would, if addressed, be subsumed in a category. However, as the essence of the problem with which we are dealing is time-based, we feel it appropriate to single out these implied terms for specific treatment.

We identify below two scenarios where the duration of the contract in question will have a direct bearing on the Year 2000 analysis. To some extent, both of these straddle two separate but intertwined categories of implied terms, namely those implied to reflect the clear intentions of the parties and those implied to supplement the recorded terms of a contract in order to make the contract commercially viable. A contract may fail if its basis is sufficiently unclear. However, the courts will do what they reasonably can to supplement gaps in an otherwise workable contract. We discussed the issue of the duration of software licences in Chapter 9. In the case of new contracts, the Year 2000 should be addressed specifically; the issue of appropriate provisions is dealt with in Chapter 9 and a form of model warranty is included at Appendix D. In that context we were dealing with software licences of fixed duration. In the context of implied terms, it is only relevant to consider licences of unspecified duration.

Is there a Liability Cut-off Date related to the Date of Supply?
There has been much debate as to whether there is a certain cut-off date which exonerates all software providers from any Year 2000 compliance obligation in respect of software provided prior to that date but renders suppliers liable regarding any software provided subsequent to that date.

There is no such simple answer. If the duration of a software licence is unspecified, the court will have to imply a term fixing the duration of the licence before assessing whether the software in question should have been made in such a way as to make it impervious to the Year 2000.

The necessity for deriving an implied term of duration of a licence of an unspecified term is that this determination is a prerequisite to the general analysis of the licensor's responsibilities to have made or make the relevant software Year 2000 compliant.

If the parties at the time of the grant of licence could not reasonably have anticipated that the software would still have been in use in the Year 2000, then it would be unfair to impose any Year 2000 compliance obligations on the licensor. However, the obverse is of course also true, namely that if the parties would reasonably have anticipated the use of the product beyond the turn of the century, then one must apply the other principles examined in this chapter in order to assess the obligations of the supplier to make the software Year 2000 compliant.

Factors Relevant in implying the Duration of a Licence of Unspecified Duration.

- The date when the software was written or sold. This is obviously going to be one of the relevant criteria. Much may hinge on the 'Clapham Omnibus' principle on which lawyers are so keen. In short, what might the reasonable user have expected of the software at the time that he acquired it? For example, if the software was sold in 1975, is it reasonable for the user to assert that the software which it bought 25 years ago should still be fit for its purpose 25 years later or was it implicit that the software had a limited lifespan? The reverse of that coin is whether the author or supplier should have had the Millennium change in mind at the time of writing or 'selling' the software.

- Platform and Functionality. The analysis will in each case also be affected by the functionality of the software and the type of platform for which the software was written. For example, if the software was written for one of the early PCs to deal with conversions from imperial to metric, it may be reasonable to infer that it would no longer be in use at the turn of the century, by which time everyone should have adapted fully to the new measurements. However, to play devil's advocate, one might consider a mainframe mortgage management software program which a building society commissioned a software house to create in 1976. In view of the fact that a mortgage written in 1976 could run its course until (say) 2001, one could certainly argue that the software should have had Year 2000 factored into it.

Year 2000 no Excuse for Failure of Service Providers

If a user has entered into a contract with an outsourcer or maintainer, which extends beyond the Year 2000 but does not refer to it, can the service provider cite the advent of the Year 2000 as a legitimate cause for interruption to or failure of that service. The terms of the contract in question will always be key, especially the liability limitation provisions. Leaving this point to one side, the simple and general answer would seem to be that if a service provider has guaranteed a service level, then the advent of the Year 2000 during the period of the contract will not absolve it from maintaining that service level. Hence, one could say that in the absence of any express terms in such contract addressing the Year 2000, the courts would be likely to imply a term into the contract that the service in question included whatever was necessary to make it impervious to Year 2000.

Terms implied by Statute other than Warranties

Various terms implied by statute could assist a user facing Year 2000 difficulties. These are set out in outline below. Whether these would help any particular user would need to be considered in detail in the light of each particular contractual situation.

The Right to correct Errors in Software

This right might well extend to enabling a user to correct Year 2000 non-compliance of software. Unfortunately, from the user's point of view, this right can be excluded by the express terms of a contract.

The Right to make a Back-up Copy of Software

This is in any event a highly advisable practice. Where one is intending to modify a software product in order to endeavour to make it Year 2000 compliant, this is all the more so.

The Right of a Lawful User of a Program to decompile it for the Purpose of creating an Interfacing Program

This right which cannot be excluded by a contractual term could be used in the context of creating a solution to certain non-compliance problems. The right may be precluded by the licensor making the interface co-ordinates of the software program 'readily available'.

The Legal Nature of Software – Goods or Software?

Before we consider the warranties implied by statute into contracts for the provision of software, we must tackle, at least in outline, the vexed legal debate as to the legal nature of software.

It may surprise the reader to know that the law has failed to categorize software definitively as goods or services. As most of the relevant law in this area distinguishes between goods and services and does not cater separately for the concept of software, the categorization of software is vital in determining the applicability of implied warranties in the context of Year 2000 as well as associated legal issues. Ideally, the law would stipulate which implied warranties are applicable to software licences. However, this is not the case and we must therefore preface the consideration of the implied warranties themselves with a consideration of how the law pertaining to goods and services is interpreted to deal with the concept of software.

Factors relevant to the Legal Categorization of Software

The factors examined below by no means constitute a comprehensive list of what is relevant to judicial determination in any particular case. As this is such an uncertain area, the indications are for general guidance only and the exact circumstances would have to be considered in every case before forming a view as to the likely categorization of the software in question.

The Mode of Delivery

If software is delivered via a modem link with the result

that there is no physical delivery, this points to the nature of that software being regarded as services. If on the other hand, software is delivered on disks which are loaded into the licensee's system and retained by the licensee, this is more akin to goods. If the disks are removed by the licensor after loading onto the licensee's system, the position is particularly murky. It will become apparent to the reader that if it has a choice in terms of mode of delivery of a software program, the choice which it makes may affect its subsequent legal rights.

Shrink-wrapped Software

This is more akin to goods as it is a standard product which one can 'buy' in the same manner in which one would buy many other items.

Bespoke Software

Software which is specially written for a customer is more akin to services.

Joint Delivery of Goods and Software

Where a user is receiving a combination of goods and software, for example a computer with various software programs pre-loaded onto it, the totality, including the software, is likely to be considered as goods.

Warranties Implied by Statute

Introduction

The law implies a warranty into a contract for the provision of professional services, such as maintenance, facilities management, outsourcing, software development or Year 2000 solution provision to the effect that the service provider must use 'reasonable care and skill' in the provision of its services. However, it imposes far heavier obligations on the suppliers of goods, namely that the goods which they supply are of 'satisfactory quality' and 'fit for the purpose' for which they were supplied. Although in this section, we shall concentrate on the applicability of the implied warranties to software, the implied warranties of 'merchantable/satisfactory quality' and 'fitness for purpose' will also be relevant in determining cases relating to the non-compliance of computers and machinery containing embedded chips.

Services and the Implied Warranty of Reasonable Skill and Care

We set out below some examples of where this warranty might be considered relevant by a court in assessing the liability of a service provider in the context of the Year 2000 in respect of services provided to a fictional company by the name of 'Y2Co Limited'.

Y2Co's offices are located on the 72nd floor of a skyscraper and Y2Co is a party to a contract with a lift maintenance company which fails to realize that the lift contains an embedded chip. At the start of Year 2000, problems with the embedded chip cause the lift to fail and Y2Co's business is adversely affected.

Y2Co appointed a facilities manager in 1997 on a fixed term five-year contract. The duties of the facilities manager included taking appropriate steps on behalf of Y2Co in relation to Year 2000. The facilities manager sent out a questionnaire to Y2Co's licensors but failed to take further action based on the responses or lack of them. Moreover the facilities manager failed to assess the Year 2000 compliance of the PCs under its control. In the Year 2000, Y2Co suffers enormous problems on account of the non-compliance of two software packages and half of Y2Co's PCs. On investigation it turns out that the facilities manager had not updated its records and its questionnaire to the licensor of one of the affected packages had never been received by that licensor. The licensor of the other package had replied that its software was not Year 2000 compliant but that an upgrade to make it compliant was available at a modest cost. The facilities manager did not act on this information or inform Y2Co of the availability of the update.

A programmer commissioned by Y2Co to write a software package in 1992 failed to make it Year 2000 compliant.

Goods and the Implied Warranty of Merchantable/Satisfactory Quality

In 1995 the term 'satisfactory quality' replaced the term 'merchantable quality' which may be more familiar to readers and which still applies to contracts entered into pre-1995. Although there are subtle differences between the two terms, we shall consider them together.

This warranty is implied only into contracts where the goods in question were supplied in the course of business. Thus a one-off sale by a consumer would not be affected.

The test to establish what constitutes merchantable or satisfactory quality is objective but takes into account the attendant circumstances. It centres on whether the goods in question are as fit for the purposes for which such goods are commonly supplied as is reasonable to expect in the circumstances, including the price and any description. The statutory replacement of the word 'satisfactory' for 'merchantable' was accompanied by the clarification that the assessment of the quality of goods may encompass, amongst other matters, their freedom from minor defects and durability.

At this stage, we can only speculate how the concepts of 'minor defects' and/or 'limited durability' might affect a software user in framing an action against a supplier in relation to a software product which proves not to be Year 2000 compliant. Users should note that if they are given a product to examine in advance of entering an agreement to acquire it, and the inspection should have revealed Year 2000 non-compliance, then the implied warranty will not apply.

One can not make a blanket statement that all software and hardware which is not Year 2000 compliant fails the satisfactory quality test. Various factors would be relevant in assessing this in respect of each set of circumstances. These include those cited above as well as the date of the licence (or other contract granting rights) as discussed in this chapter under 'Implied Terms' where the nature of the terms implied as to the duration of a licence of unspecified length was addressed.

We can conclude our analysis of the merchantable/satisfactory quality implied term by reiterating that this places a more onerous burden on a supplier than that imposed by the 'reasonable skill and care' test which applies to services provision. Thus, even if a supplier of goods used reasonable skill and care, this would not necessarily mean that the goods supplied pass muster for the purposes of the merchantable/satisfactory quality test. In the recent case of *St Albans v ICL*, the court indicated that the distinction between the implied warranties relating to services and goods should be eliminated in the context of software. However, to date this has not happened.

Goods and the Implied Warranty of Fitness for a Particular Purpose

If a potential customer makes known expressly or by implication to a potential supplier its reason for wishing to acquire certain goods, then, unless the customer did not rely or should not have relied on the supplier's expertize, the law implies a term into the contract that the goods are reasonably fit for that purpose.

Let us hypothesize that in 1995 an observatory commissioned a software house to provide it with a telescope incorporating software which would enable it to record planetary movements and explained to the software house that its main interest was in a planetary eclipse that was due to take place in 2004. If the software house failed to make the software Year 2000 compliant and as a result it was unable accurately to record the details of the eclipse, this could well be a case where Year 2000 non-compliance constituted a breach of the warranty for a particular purpose. Of course, this would pre-suppose that the software in question was categorized as an item of goods.

Finally, readers should note that this warranty also comes into play only where the goods in question are supplied in the course of business.

LIMITATION AND EXCLUSION OF CONTRACTUAL LIABILITY

General

One of the common threads of legal systems throughout the world is that parties who have engaged themselves contractually are bound by the terms of the contract into which they have entered and that the role of the courts in contractual matters is to preserve contractually created rights and enforce contractually created obligations. Accordingly, in English law, the general principle is that any person is free to bind himself by any contractual commitment he chooses to make. This principle is however not sacrosanct and is tempered in various ways where there are issues at stake which are considered to outweigh the importance of the doctrine of the inviolability of the contract.

Certain of these factors are considered so fundamental that they actually prevent the formation of the contract or vitiate it entirely. These factors cluster around the concepts of the incapacity of one or more of the parties, the illegality of the subject-matter of the contract or the repugnance of the contract to principles of public policy. There are also external factors which come into play, which do not affect the formation or existence of a contract but have an effect on the provisions of the contract. These factors also stem from considerations of public policy such as the protection of the consumer and the striking out of unfair bargains.

It is against this backdrop that one must consider contracts dealing with the provision of goods or services which seek to limit and/or exclude the potential liability of the supplier for losses sustained by the customer as a direct or indirect result of the contractual relationship.

Indeed, it is rare to find a supply contract which does not seek to exclude the potential liability of the supplier for various types of loss which might be sustained by the customer and which does not additionally seek to limit any damages which the supplier must pay out in the event that the exclusions are ineffective. Contracts relating to the supply of hardware, software, machinery containing embedded chips and the provision of services in relation to any of these items are no exception.

The crucial question for our purposes is how effective such clauses of limitation and exclusion will be in protecting suppliers against claims by customers who suffer losses in the context of the Year 2000 on account of the non-compliance of systems or the inability of service providers to comply with their service provision obligations.

Before we turn in more detail to the question of the effectiveness of such clauses, it is important that the reader appreciates that it may be unnecessary to consider this issue if the clauses have not been successfully incorporated by the supplier into the contract or the contract containing such clauses has been terminated due to a fundamental contractual breach by the party seeking to invoke the clauses. The issues of incorporation of terms into contracts and fundamental breach are dealt with by all the standard textbooks on the law of contract but are not the focus of this book. However these matters should be considered by parties to a contractual dispute in assessing the strength of their respective cases.

The Effectiveness of Contractual Clauses which purport to Limit and/or Exclude the Contractual Liability of a Provider of Goods or Services

There are various factors, principles and laws applied by the courts in limiting the effect of such clauses. We will now examine those which we consider to be the most important in the context of Year 2000. In each case, we will give a hypothetical example of the potential relevance to Year 2000 disputes.

In this context we must remind the reader of the discussion earlier in this chapter relating to the difficulties which the law has in determining whether the nature of software is more akin to goods or services.

Exclusion and Liability Clauses which are automatically invalid under the Unfair Contract Terms Act 1977

Clauses purporting to limit or exclude the Liability of a Supplier to a 'Consumer' for Breach of the Implied Terms as to Merchantable/Satisfactory Quality or Fitness for Purpose

In this context, the law attributes a particular meaning to the term 'consumer'. For our purposes, this situation arises where one party to a contract acts in the course of business but the other does not and does not hold itself out as doing so.

This might be relevant where Mr Smith, a sports-enthusiast, bought a video recorder in 1998 from an electrical retailer having first informed the salesman that he wanted a good one so as to be able to relive the highlights of the 1998 World Cup and the 2000 Olympics. The salesman suggested a particular model, which in the event turns out not to be Year 2000 compliant and packs up at the start of the Year 2000.

Clauses purporting to limit or exclude the Liability of a Supplier for Death or Personal Injury resulting from Negligence
This might be relevant in the event that a patient died because of a malfunction in a dialysis machine supplied to a hospital in 1998 by a medical instruments company that had omitted to check whether the embedded chip which controlled the operation of the machine was Year 2000 compliant.

Clauses purporting to limit or exclude the Liability of a Supplier for Breach of the Term of Quiet Possession
This relates to a warranty implied by statute into contracts relating to the supply of goods. Without entering into detail, this type of implied term might be relevant to prevent the licensor of a standard software package preventing the licensee from fixing the non-compliance of the software by asserting that this would constitute an infringement of copyright.

Exclusion and Liability Clauses which are invalid under the Unfair Contract Terms Act 1977 unless they are reasonable

Clauses purporting to limit or exclude the Liability of a Supplier to a 'Non-consumer' for Breach of the Implied Terms as to Merchantable/Satisfactory Quality or Fitness for Purpose
Let us take the case of Mr Smith. He is a director of a company which supplies video excerpts from important sporting events. In 1998, he bought a video recorder from an electrical retailer having first informed the salesman that he wanted a good one so as to be able to offer customers highlights of the 1998 World Cup and the 2000 Olympics. The

salesman suggested a particular model, which in the event turns out not to be Year 2000 compliant and packs up at the start of the Year 2000.

Clauses purporting to limit or exclude the Liability of a Supplier for Breach of Contract in a transaction where the Customer is either a 'Consumer' or deals on the Supplier's Standard Terms of Business

In this case, the concept of exclusion and limitation of liability clauses is extended to cover clauses by which the supplier is entitled to render a contractual performance substantially different from that which was reasonably expected of him, or to tender no performance at all in respect of the whole or any or all of its contractual obligations. This might be relevant where a packaged software retailer has committed itself contractually to supply a particular software package to a customer but on failing to do so points out to the customer a term in its standard terms of business which allows it to 'substitute an alternative software package for any which we have contracted to supply even if the alternative package has inferior functionality'.

Clauses purporting to limit or exclude the Liability of a Supplier for Misrepresentations made prior to a Contract

This might be relevant where the salesman in the earlier example told Mr Smith when he was deciding whether to buy the video suggested by the salesman that the video would give trouble-free service for at least 10 years.

Clauses purporting to limit or exclude the Liability of a Supplier for Negligence where the Customer suffers Loss or Damage other than Death or Personal Injury

This might be relevant in the event that a hospital had to buy a replacement machine because of a malfunction in a dialysis machine supplied to it in 1998 by a medical instruments company which had omitted to check whether the embedded chip which controlled the operation of the machine was Year 2000 compliant.

Reasonableness

As the fate of the types of exclusion and limitation clauses set out above depends on whether they are deemed to be reasonable, consideration must be given as to what a court is likely to consider reasonable.

This is not a simple matter and in addition to statutory guidance, there is much relevant caselaw on this topic. A detailed analysis of this issue is outside the remit of this work. However, the principal factors likely to be considered by a court in this analysis include the following:

- whether the goods were supplied to the special order of the customer
- the respective abilities of the parties to bear the loss
- inducements received by the customer to agree to the limitation or exclusion of liability
- whether at the time the contract was entered into, the supplier could reasonably have been expected to fulfil the contractual obligation in respect of which liability is excluded or limited
- the existence of alternative sources of supply
- the customer's knowledge of the relevant limitation or exclusion
- the contractual bargaining power of the parties
- the level of complexity involved in the supplier's performance of the subject-matter of the limitation or exclusion.

OTHER LEGAL ISSUES LIKELY TO BE RELEVANT IN THE CONTEXT OF THE RESOLUTION OF YEAR 2000 DISPUTES

Non-derogation From Grant

This legal principle of 'non-derogation from grant' is the legal formulation of the concept that a party cannot take away with one hand what it has given with the other. This principle could be relevant in the Year 2000 context in relation to the position of a licensee of software who knows that the software in question is non-compliant. Having unsuccessfully approached the supplier with a request that the software be made compliant, the user finds itself faced with the following options:

- abandoning the software altogether
- continuing to use the software and risking the consequences of non-compliance
- trying to fix it itself
- procuring the services of a Year 2000 solution provider to fix it.

In many cases, the first two options are economically unacceptable and the third is beyond the technical capabilities of the user. Thus, only the fourth option is realistic for the user. However, allowing the necessary access to the software to a third party might well infringe the terms of the software licence. The principle of non-derogation might be applied in this context to save the user from this 'Catch 22'. The argument would have to run along the following lines. The user has been granted a licence to use the software. In order to be able to continue to use the software, it needs to make the software Year 2000 compliant. Without the assistance of a third party, it cannot make the software Year 2000 compliant. Therefore to deny it the right to have the software modified by a third party would constitute a derogation from the right to use the software granted by the software licence.

Force Majeure

One often finds such a clause near the end of an agreement. Whilst the exact parameters of such clauses vary from contract to contract, they basically exclude the liability of one party or both parties for acts which are unforeseeable and beyond their reasonable control. Invariably, this includes acts of God, but the ambit is often extended to matters such as strikes and illness. The question has been asked whether Year 2000 might be considered an instance of force majeure, thereby excluding the liability of a supplier of services, or possibly goods, in the event that the supply is interrupted on account of its inability to service the requirements of the customer for reasons associated with its own non-compliance or that of entities higher up in the supply chain on which it depends.

As the potential Year 2000 problems which are the topic of this book are now so clearly in the public focus, it is unlikely that a force majeure clause which did not expressly include the Year 2000 would serve to exonerate a supplier that let down one or more customers. However, for the avoidance of doubt, in relation to any contracts which the reader enters as a customer, it is recommended that it should expressly exclude the advent of the Year 2000 from the ambit of force majeure clauses.

Frustration

Frustration arises where without default of either party to the contract, a contractual obligation has become incapable of being performed because the circumstances in which performance is called for would render it a thing radically different from that which was envisaged by the contract.

The basic effect of frustration is to discharge the parties from their contractual obligations. The foreseeability of the Year 2000 makes it unlikely that a service provider acting under a contract which is silent as to the Year 2000 but whose general contractual obligations would make it necessary for it to make the subject-matter of the contract Year

2000 compliant would be able successfully to argue frustration to absolve it from such liability.

However, in the interests of caution, in relation to any contracts that the reader enters as a customer, it might wish to include in the contract an express term to the effect that the advent of the Year 2000 will not result in the frustration of the contract.

Estoppel

If one party to a contract has been brought under an incorrect impression (ie misled) by the other party, and in reliance on that impression the second party has acted to its detriment, the second party may prevent the first party from relying on the correct state of affairs before a court of law. This doctrine might be relevant in various Year 2000-related scenarios.

Let us take the example of a software house that receives a questionnaire from one of its software licensees enquiring as to the Year 2000 compliance status of the software and the software house replied that it would make the software 'fully compliant well in advance of the Millennium through the supply of a free update'. The licensee relies on this assurance and tells its Year 2000 solution provider not to fix that particular software product. In the event, the software is not made Year 2000 compliant by the software house and the licensee suffers considerable losses. In these circumstances, the software house might be estopped from claiming that it is not liable for those losses because it had never guaranteed the Year 2000 compliance of the software.

To this extent, the doctrine of estoppel where applied can provide an exception to the entire agreement concept discussed earlier in this chapter as it can effectively produce an alteration to the terms of the contract by virtue of a statement that did not form part of the contract. The normal contractual requirement of consideration would also need to be addressed in this context.

Ambiguity or Lack of Clarity

In the event that a contractual clause is considered by a court to be either unclear or ambiguous, the court will typically interpret the area of uncertainty in favour of the customer. In the Year 2000 context, this is most likely to be applicable in the interpretation of clauses purporting to limit or exclude the liability of a supplier.

Contract Law

Remedies for Breach of Contract – Recovering damages and other forms of relief against the suppliers who cause your problems

INTRODUCTION

Many predictions abound as to the catastrophic effects of the advent of the Year 2000 and various other date changes on the functionality and performance of software, hardware and machinery containing embedded chips. Whilst a minority are still contemptuous of the media coverage as hype, there are very few informed people who would seriously dispute that many companies will suffer enormous losses as a result of these technical problems and that a substantial percentage of those will seek to recover their losses via litigation and other forms of dispute resolution.

In Chapter 17, we will deal with the topic of limitation of actions, whereby a party can find itself out of time to make a legal claim. Limitation may thus prevent an entity which suffers loss on account of Year 2000 from succeeding in an action against the party responsible for causing that loss. Although the matter has, of course, not yet been determined by the courts of England and Wales in the context of Year 2000, it seems clear that in respect of a claim based on a breach of contract, the limit is six years from the date of provision of the software. This means that anyone waiting to sue till Year 2000 will be out of time in respect of any software acquired before the relevant date in 1994. The problem inherent in this situation is that many users will only become aware of the problems resident in their software, hardware and embedded chip-containing machinery once they are already out of time to sue in contract.

Where one finds oneself prevented by virtue of limitation or other matters from pursuing a contractual action, one might be able to initiate an action in tort on the basis of negligence. The measure of damages available is different from that in an action based on contract and this is considered below. The possibility of founding actions in tort on the basis of Year 2000-related problems is considered in Chapter 12.

In Chapter 10, we alluded to the problems which can arise as to the determination of the law which is applicable to the resolution of a particular dispute in relation to contracts where all the relevant parties and factors are not located in the same country.

For the purposes of this chapter, we are limiting ourselves to cases where there are no problems in relation to the applicable law or limitation periods.

In principle, there are various forms of legal remedy available in the event that one suffers contractual losses. Predominant amongst these is damages. However, we will also consider other remedies which might be available to an entity suffering loss directly or indirectly on account of the advent of the Year 2000.

DAMAGES

In this context, there are two avenues of potential legal recourse against suppliers of non-compliant software, hardware or machinery comprising embedded chips. The first relates to the costs of remedying the defective item and could be recoverable now. The second relates to losses resulting from the use of non-compliant products and may well be for loss of profits arising after the Year 2000.

The chances of recovering damages for any losses suffered will depend on whether there are any express terms in the contract imposing responsibility for supplying compliant systems or curing non-compliance. In the absence of any express terms, the user will be forced to fall back on terms implied by law as considered in Chapter 10. It may also be possible to rely on pre-contractual representations made by the supplier if these have not been effectively excluded by the contract itself. In this context, the reader is referred back to the sections on entire agreement clauses, estoppel and the limitation and exclusion of liability in Chapter 10.

In the event that a party to a contract is able to establish that another party to that contract is responsible for damage which it has suffered in the context of the Year 2000, it does not follow automatically that the innocent party will be able to recover all the losses which it suffers on account of that damage. The chances of recovery will be affected by various factors. Prevalent amongst these is the interaction of the likely judicial categorization of the loss sustained with the categories of loss excluded or limited by the express terms of the relevant contract. There are also other factors which may act to delimit the damages which one party may recover from another and these are considered below.

Thus, before we consider the Year 2000-related losses which a customer might recover from a supplier of goods or services which directly or indirectly caused losses to that customer, we must consider how such losses are legally categorized and the concept of remoteness.

Categories of Loss and Damage

Terminology is used loosely in this area; the terms 'damage' and 'loss' being used almost interchangeably. Losses are traditionally categorized as either direct, indirect or consequential. Whereas the terms 'direct losses' and 'indirect losses' are generally used to refer to losses which are physical in nature, the term 'consequential losses', which is synonomous with 'economic losses' usually relates to loss of profits.

In the context of Year 2000 non-compliant software, this categorization might be applied to a dispute in the following way:

- direct loss – the cost of replacing or repairing the software
- indirect loss – the cost of replacing or repairing a hard disk which crashes on account of the software problems
- consequential/economic loss – the loss of profits incurred by the licensee by reason of being unable to service its own clients' requirements on account of the defective software.

Factors which may have an Impact on the Damages awarded in the Context of Year 2000

The basic principle in actions for damages based upon a breach of contract is that damages are awarded to put the innocent party in the same position as it would have been in if the contract had been performed. However, the award and determination of the level of damages in any case are subject to various factors, including the effect of limitation and exclusion of liability clauses as discussed above and the qualifications set out below.

Remoteness

The law cannot hold a party to a contract liable for all the detrimental consequences of his breach of contract. Damage which, though factually caused by the breach, is too remote in the eyes of the law to attract liability, should not be compensated.

In determining where to draw the line between damages which are not too remote and those which are, the courts have generally applied the test of foreseeability of consequences. In other words, if the losses resulting from a breach were of a type which could reasonably have been foreseen by the parties at the time of entering the contract they are recoverable. This is so even if the extent of such losses could not reasonably have been foreseen.

If the parties to a contract were involved in pre-contractual discussions, the likelihood of the vendor/licensor of a non-compliant software program/piece of machinery being aware of the potential licensee's/purchaser's plans for the product and hence being able to foresee the type of losses which the licensee/purchaser would suffer in the event of non-compliance are greatly increased. In such intimate circumstances, the exposure of the supplier to damages is typically far greater than in cases where, at least pre-contractually, the parties are unknown to each other.

It follows that a potential customer/licensee would be well advised to inform a potential supplier/licensor of the potential losses it would suffer in the event of Year 2000 non-compliance of the item in question.

Mitigation

It is usually said that a party to a contract who suffers damage as a result of breach of contract has a duty to mitigate his damage. In mitigating his loss, a party to a contract is expected to take the steps a reasonable man in his position would have taken. The reasonableness of the conduct in mitigation will be considered with reference to all the circumstances of a case. If the matter goes to court, it is for the defendant to prove any allegation it makes regarding the plaintiff's failure to mitigate.

Failure to mitigate loss will generally result in a diminution in the level of damages awarded. If a party has incurred expenses in taking reasonable steps to mitigate his loss, he should in principle be able to recover such expenses from the party in breach as part of his damages.

It is not difficult to see how this principle might be applicable in the context of Year 2000. Let us consider the case of a licensee of a software package which the licensee knows not to be Year 2000 compliant despite the presence of a warranty in the licence to the effect that it is totally compliant. The licensee knows that if the software is not made compliant it will suffer enormous losses and its business may actually fail. It therefore invites the software house to make the software compliant. The software house declines, replying that the package is fine. The licensee has 3 options:

- waiting for the Year 2000 and seeing what harm the non-compliant software causes – as mentioned above, the consequences may be fatal
- engaging the services of a third party to render the software compliant – the estimated cost is £10,000
- replacing the software with a competitive package which the licensee knows to be Year 2000 compliant – the cost would be £25,000.

If the licensee followed the first course, he would leave himself open to the defence that he failed to take reasonable steps to mitigate his loss and any damages that he recovered would be reduced accordingly to exclude damages for the loss which he could have avoided through mitigation.

If the licensee followed the second course, then as long as he could establish subsequently that the software was not originally compliant, he should be able to recover the £10,000.

If the licensee followed the third course, then the software house could argue that the licensee could have mitigated cost more effectively by adopting the second course, and argue for a proportional reduction in the award to the licensee. However, it should be noted in this context that such an argument would probably be unsuccessful as the law imposes no obligation to determine the cheapest available method of mitigation.

Novus Actus Interveniens

The chain of causation between the breach of contract and the damage suffered must remain intact. If the defendant can establish that an intervening event broke that chain, then he should be able to avoid any liability. In this context it should be noted that it seems that reasonable acts by the plaintiff will not be held to break the chain of causation.

Let us take the example of a diagnostic machine purchased by a hospital in 1998. In the contract of sale, the supplier warranted that the machine 'will work without interruption or defect until at least 2008'. In 1998, the hospital does some tests which reveal that the machine is not Year-2000 compliant and will be rendered worthless in the Year 2000. The hospital contacts the supplier who says he will fix it and a date is fixed for the supplier to carry out the remedial work. Before the appointed date, there is a change in the hospital administration and the new administrator gets in an old friend who claims to be a Year 2000 expert to fix the machine. This so-called Year 2000 expert is so inexpert that he wrecks the machine to the extent that it cannot be repaired. Thus the causal link between the non-compliance of the machine and its ultimate worthlessness is broken.

Disproportionate Cost of Repair

If a contract obliges the supplier or maintainer to make a product Year 2000 compliant, then the user should be able to recover the internal and external expenses and costs it incurs in making that product compliant, or, if this is not viable, the cost of a replacement product.

However, if the non-compliance of a given product will produce only relatively minor loss of amenity to the user, then a court may determine that the damages awarded should not be on a full replacement basis but rather reflect the loss of amenity in the context as a proportion of the overall benefit which the user was entitled to derive under the terms of the contract.

Expenses not related to Breach of Contract

Certain expenses incurred by a user in the context of determining whether its systems are Year 2000 compliant may not be recoverable even if it discovers non-compliance in certain elements of its infrastructure. The reason is that these expenses are not caused by the breach of contract; they would have been incurred by the user even if its systems had proved to be fully compliant.

Where the services of Year 2000 solution providers have been engaged, it may count against the user if it does not offer the first opportunity to fix non-compliance problems to the supplier of the relevant product.

SPECIFIC PERFORMANCE

This remedy is somewhat secondary, consisting in a power of the courts to order parties to carry out contractual obligations; but only where damages would not be an adequate remedy and where the obligations are not complex in nature. It is considered unlikely that this remedy will play a large role in the context of Year 2000 as damages should be an adequate remedy and the fixing of Year 2000 problems may be intrinsically quite complex.

However, there may be instances where what is required for Year 2000 compliance is the supply of an item which is already in existence and held by the supplier. In such a scenario, specific performance might be both appropriate and available.

TERMINATION

In certain cases, a user of a product which is not Year 2000 compliant may be able to terminate the contract under which the product was supplied and to reject the product. However, these rights may be lost if the user either continues to use the goods after discovering the non-compliance or fails to exercise the rights promptly.

Due to the expected time lag in most cases between supply and ascertainment of non-compliance, it is thought unlikely that many users will be able to avail themselves of this right in the context of Year 2000.

Termination may however be a viable option in service provision contracts such as maintenance or facilities management if the service provider is contractually obliged to eliminate non-compliance but fails to do so. The timing of such termination would be very important; with undue haste or delay bringing undesirable consequences for the user.

Tort

If others have caused us loss through their negligent actions or statements, what are our legal rights?

INTRODUCTION

When we speak about tort in the Year 2000 context, what we are fundamentally discussing is the tort of negligence which relates to the harm that one entity can cause to another through its negligent conduct. By and large, a party is only likely to start an action in tort if it has no realistic option of doing so in contract.

REASONS FOR SUING IN CONTRACT RATHER THAN TORT

Measure of Damages

There are differences between contract and tort in relation to the measure of damages and the categories of loss for which damages are available.

Whereas in contract, a plaintiff, if successful, can expect

to recover not only his losses but also his lost profits, in tort he can only expect to recover his losses. Furthermore, in tort a plaintiff is unlikely to recover economic losses which it suffers unless they are a consequence of physical damage or, in certain circumstances, result from a negligent misstatement by the defendant.

There is a somewhat anomalous dichotomy in negligence actions depending on whether the basis of the tort was an act or a statement. The essence of the dichotomy is that economic losses which are not related to physical damage are generally not recoverable in tort but may be if the tort was a misstatement. In the Year 2000 context, there is the potential for this distinction to have a significant effect on damages awards.

Let us take the example of a non-compliant word processing software program which causes sporadic omissions from documents on printing. This software is used in January 2000 to produce a prospectus for the stock market listing of a company. At this stage, nobody is aware of the non-compliance. Because of the defect, the prospectus, when printed, omits details of the dubious background of one of the directors. Various investors who would have been put off by the director's track record put money into the company. The company goes into receivership after six months when it is discovered that the director has been embezzling. The investors want to sue the software house in negligence for having produced a non-compliant software package.

If the incomplete prospectus can be characterized as a negligent misstatement, the investors may be successful in their action. Otherwise, they will not.

Sustaining Damage

In the discussion of limitation periods in Chapter 10, we noted that the trigger in tort is the date of the damage caused by the software whereas in contract it is probably the date of supply of the software. We also observed that this may lead to a party finding itself out of time in contract before it realizes that it has a claim. It follows from this that an action in tort must be predicated on the occurrence of damage whereas this is not the case in contract.

Thus, in the Year 2000 context, it would be likely to prove very difficult or even impossible to recover in tort the costs of remedial work carried out on non-compliant software on a preventative basis whereas in contract it would not.

Standard of Proof

There is a marked difference between actions in tort and contract based on the supply of allegedly defective goods. Whereas a plaintiff in a claim based in tort (ie negligence) must establish that the defendant failed to act with 'reasonable skill and care', this is not necessary in contract where, irrespective of its level of skill and care, the defendant might still be held liable on the basis of failure to discharge the implied warranties of fitness for purpose and merchantable/satisfactory quality discussed in Chapter 10.

REASONS FOR SUING IN TORT RATHER THAN CONTRACT

Limitation Periods

In Chapter 17 (on dispute resolution) we discuss the limitation periods which may make it possible to start an action in tort when one is already outside the contractual limitation periods.

It is worth adding here that in respect of claims for personal injury caused by negligence, the limitation period is only three years. Let us take an example where Year 2000 could play a role. A lift maintenance company which knows that the lift which it is maintaining contains a chip which is not Year 2000 compliant considers itself liable for making the lift compliant. The replacement of the chip necessitates dismantling of the lift and the reassembly is negligent, ultimately causing the lift to plummet to the bottom of the shaft severely injuring several people.

Absence of Contractual Relationship

The doctrine of privity of contract means that a contract only creates rights and obligations between the parties to that contract. Thus, in general terms, a third party cannot sue or be sued on the basis of a contract. Whereas in tort, before the tort is perpetrated, the parties are often not bound to each other in any way and may well be completely unknown to one another. Thus, if in the Year 2000 context, one had been wronged by an entity with which one had no contractual relationship, one's only option would be to sue in tort.

Let us consider for example a retail company which commissioned a software house in 1997 to write a software program to label its products with 'best before dates'. The retailer was well informed and the contract with the software house contained a clause whereby the software house warranted the Year 2000 compliance of the software. The software house engaged external contractors on a short term basis to write the program.

The Year 2000 arrives and the software is not compliant. The retailer loses considerable custom as consumers discover that the 'best before date' labels on items on sale in the retailer's shops do not make sense; some listing dates in 1900.

The retailer's best option would have been to sue the software house. Unfortunately, the software house has gone out of business. The remaining option is to sue the programmer who, it could be argued, was negligent in writing software which was not Year 2000 compliant. As the retailer has no contract with the programmer, it cannot sue him in contract and is only left with the tortious avenue.

DUTY

Existence of a Duty

In both contract and tort, a duty must have been owed to the party sustaining the damage by the party which caused the damage. In the case of a contract, the duty arises from the terms of the contract. In tort, in somewhat simplistic terms, the duty arises if the party causing the damage could reasonably have foreseen that the party suffering the damage would suffer damage as a result of the first party's negligence. The greater the 'proximity' of the parties, the more likely it is that this tortious duty will arise.

Proximity

Thus, if in the example cited earlier, the programmer knew the identity of the retailer and for what ends it required the software, this would probably be sufficient to establish such a duty.

The chance of such a duty arising in the case of package software is far slighter as the programmer and the user will be far less proximate and the supplier will be unlikely to know the individual business requirements of the user. Other indications in the Year 2000 context of a relationship which is less than proximate might include the absence of a signed licence agreement or the fact that non-compliant software was downloaded from the Internet; especially if done so without charge.

If, however, a software house agrees to provide a fix to a user who might for the reasons above have previously been considered insufficiently proximate, the agreement to provide the fix may well create the previously lacking duty. Subsequent failure to remedy the non-compliance may, in turn, constitute a breach of that duty. This state of affairs might, of course, influence software houses not to offer fixes unless they are contractually bound to do so.

In the case of embedded chips, the creator of the chip is far less likely to know details of the end-user and its intended uses. Hence, the chances of establishing the existence of the necessary proximity and foreseeability would seem far slighter.

Absence of Consideration

In our analysis of actions based in contract, we discussed the need for consideration. This can be summarized as the need for each party to derive a benefit from the contract in order for breach of commitments which it has made to be actionable. In tort, however, there is no need for a party to have derived any benefit from the scenario in which the tort arose or for any relationship to have existed between the wronged party and the wronging party. Thus, the maker of a statement may owe a duty to anyone who may reasonably be foreseen as belonging to a grouping that might rely on such statement and suffer loss in the event of the statement being negligently wrong.

In the Year 2000 context, a software supplier or equipment supplier who informs its distributor that the items in question are Year 2000 compliant may well owe such a duty to the customers of such distributor as the erroneous information is likely to be passed on to them and relied upon.

Obligation to Warn?

Although it is far from clear, it is also thought that suppliers may have a duty to warn users of products which it has supplied in the past when it becomes subsequently aware of potential damage being sustained by such users. Much software and embedded chip-containing machinery in use today which is actually non-compliant was supplied without any thought of its Year 2000 compliance status. Suppliers who supplied such items may now however be fixed with a duty to warn users in relation to non-compliance.

If such a duty to warn does exist, it brings with it many questions in the Year 2000 context. For example, is it sufficient to warn users of the non-compliance without fixing it and will an inadequate warning be worse from the point of view of the supplier's potential liability than no warning at all?

Breach of Duty

Again, in both contract and tort, the duty owed must be breached to engender liability.

In tort, once it has been established in a particular set of circumstances that a supplier owed a duty to act with reasonable skill and care, the question focuses on whether the actions or omissions of the supplier breached that duty. In the Year 2000 context where an interval of several years may exist between the creation or supply of the software or embedded chip, this analysis could prove very difficult. For example, could a programmer who developed Year 2000 non-compliant software in 1990 and which worked perfectly well for ten years be said to have lacked reasonable care and skill?

The potential duty owed by a supplier to its distributor's customers may be breached if the Year 2000 compliance statement made to such distributor is in fact a negligent misstatement. We focus here on negligent misstatements rather than acts in view of the greater potential for the recovery of economic losses, a fact which is likely to be very important in the Year 2000 context.

If indeed suppliers are under a duty to give a warning of Year 2000 non-compliance in respect of products which they have supplied, then failure to do so would constitute a breach. In fact, as discussed above, for a duty to arise in tort, there is no requirement that the parties know of each other but a certain proximity must exist.

Concurrent Liability in Negligence and Contract

We have discussed some of the differences between and similarities of actions in contract and tort. The interaction of these two branches of the law becomes evident when one realises that the fact that two parties have entered into a contract does not mean that they cannot sue one another in tort.

It is quite possible to breach a contract and commit a tort simultaneously. In our discussion of implied warranties in Chapter 10, we considered the implied warranty of reasonable skill and care which arises in relation to the provision of services. If one considers that negligence arises where one party owes a duty of skill and care to another which it has failed to acquit, the link between the two branches becomes apparent. Where the same act or omission constitutes both a breach of contract and negligence, the wronged party will only be able to recover for one or the other but should, in principle, be able to choose whether to proceed in contract or tort.

This choice may however be lost through circumstances such as the expiry of the contractual limitation period. The option to choose is further hampered by the courts which, it seems, will not allow an action in tort where this avenue is being used merely to try to circumvent exclusions in a contract.

The duty to mitigate loss exists in tort as it does in contract and therefore users should act now to reduce or, hopefully, eliminate their risk exposure to the Year 2000.

Causation and Remoteness

As is the case with actions based on contract, in order for the plaintiff to recover damages, the court must be satisfied that the breach of duty caused the losses and that the losses are not too remote from the breach to merit the award of damages. The concepts of remoteness and foreseeability are inextricably linked.

In respect of both contractual and tortious claims, the courts distinguish between the foreseeability of the type of loss and the foreseeability of the extent of loss. The basic rule in both contract and tort is that if physical damage or injury is within the contemplation of the parties, recovery of damages in respect of such damage or injury will not be limited by virtue of the extent of such damage or injury being unforeseeable.

In the context of Year 2000, it may well prove very difficult in advance to assess the extent of damages that an IT user might suffer on account of a non-compliant software product. At the time of installation in (say) 1994, the software program might have been running in isolation but by the time it fails, it might have become part of an extremely intricate IT system involving many interfacing and mutually dependent products.

Obviously, the extent of the losses will generally be greater in the case of a more complex system where greater remedial work will be necessary and the dependence of the user will probably be greater. However, it is believed that the types of damage which might be suffered on account of Year 2000 failure will often be foreseeable.

The categorization of types of loss will therefore be crucial to a plaintiff's recovery prospects. The type of loss/extent of loss dichotomy can produce anomalous situations where the use of a product in a foreseeable manner but in an unforeseeable context could produce far greater losses than the use of the same product in a foreseeable manner and context. Whether the fact that losses arising in a foreseeable manner arise in an unforeseeable context is sufficient to have the losses categorized as a separate type of loss will be crucial to the level of damages awarded.

Let us take the example of a company which purchases a PC from a computer retailer in 1995. The PC is not very powerful and is of a type usually used for domestic purposes. However the purchaser uses it for its business purposes and when the PC fails, he loses all sorts of valuable client data and work in progress. Is loss of data the relevant category or are there two separate categories, namely loss of typical domestic data and loss of typical commercial data? If it is all one category, the potential damages award will be far greater. We will consider later issues such as contributory negligence which could impact on the award of damages in a case where a user has failed to back up valuable data.

Supply Chain Liability

If a user of a software product, a computer or machinery containing an embedded chip suffers damage on account of that item being Year 2000 non-compliant, the normal course of action would be to try to recover its losses from the supplier. However, if the supplier is no longer in existence or its terms of business effectively exclude its liability for the user's losses, the user's only recourse will be to look to recover its losses higher up the supply chain.

Unless the user is a consumer and able to benefit from the Consumer Protection Act mentioned below, any action against entities higher up the supply chain would have to be founded in tort. The doctrine of privity of contract precludes contractual claims against entities with which one does not have a contractual relationship.

The factors which will determine whether such a claim

might be successful have already been considered in this chapter. These include proximity of the parties, and foreseeability of type of loss. In general, the higher up the supply chain one rises, the greater the gap between the user and the potential defendant becomes and the slighter the chances that the courts will find that the necessary level of proximity exists.

Statutory Assistance for the Plaintiff

We refer to the Unfair Contract Terms Act later in this chapter in the section on defences. There are two other statutes which might assist those users who suffer on account of Year 2000 non-compliance and to which we would therefore draw the reader's attention.

Consumer Protection Act 1987

It is possible that this Act will assist private consumers in certain circumstances where they have acquired non-compliant products. If applicable, the Act will facilitate matters for a claimant as it imposes strict liability for personal injury and damage thereby dispensing the claimant from the need to prove the existence of a duty owed to it by a third party and the breach of that duty.

Where the non-compliant item in question is software, it is unclear whether the Act which refers to 'products' is applicable. Whether the software is standard or bespoke may play a role in the determination of the applicability of the Act in any particular case.

In any event, this Act will be of no assistance to businesses as it only protects private consumers.

Misrepresentation Act 1967

This statute may be of assistance to a user where it has suffered damage on account of Year 2000 non-compliance of an item and there was a negligent misrepresentation to that user before it entered the contract to the effect that the item in question was compliant.

As with the Consumer Protection Act, this Act enables a potential plaintiff to avoid the difficulties which it might otherwise experience in establishing that the defendant owed it a duty and breached that duty.

The Act also favours users in that it is up to the maker of the representation to show that it was true or that it was reasonable for him to believe it to be so. The Act applies to some but not all pre-contractual statements.

Damages awarded under this Act are assessed on the tortious rather than the contractual basis. This distinction is considered earlier in this chapter.

Defences – Partial and Total Defences to a Claim in Negligence

Novus Actus Interveniens

In our review of contract law, we noted that one of the requirements for liability is that the chain of causation between the breach of contract and the damage suffered must remain intact and that if a defendant can establish that an intervening event broke that chain, then he should be able to avoid any liability

This doctrine is equally applicable in tort. In the Year 2000 context, it might arise where a company which uses a non-compliant software program engages the services of a Year 2000 solution provider to make the software compliant but the solution provider, by tampering with the software, only makes the problem worse.

A software house which endeavoured to escape liability on the basis of this argument would almost certainly fail if a back up copy of the software were available.

State of the Art

One of the relevant factors in many Year 2000 cases is likely to be the comparison of the industry development procedure standard at the time of development of the non-compliant item with the work carried out by the developer.

In this connection, it is worth mentioning that many programmers faced with the charge of having been negligent in creating non-compliant software might well argue that the use of a two digit date field to indicate the year when writing software was considered normal practice for many years due to the lower requirements that this would place on computer memory which was, until relatively recently, far from abundant.

Although it will generally be helpful for a defendant to establish that he acted in accordance with the industry standard prevalent at the time, this will not necessarily mean that he acted with reasonable skill and care which is the acid test for negligence defences.

Contributory Negligence

The damages of a claimant will be reduced to reflect the extent to which the court considers the claimant's own negligence has contributed to the damage.

For example, if a user has been informed by a supplier that a particular machine is non-compliant but fails to act on that information and continues to use the machine regardless, this could well act to reduce the damages that the user could recover from the manufacturer. From this example, it can be seen that contributory negligence and failure to mitigate may be very closely intertwined.

Mitigation

Where a negligent act or omission constitutes the breach of a tortious duty, the party which is at the receiving end of such negligence must take reasonable steps to minimize the consequences of such breach. Failure to do so will generally result in a diminution in the level of damages awarded.

It would seem that the principle of mitigation is likely to play a large role in much of the litigation relating to Year 2000 as many users who are aware of potential problems with products which they are using are doing nothing about such problems. Appropriate mitigating acts might include procuring fixes or obtaining replacements or, in the case of software, the appointment of a Year 2000 solution provider.

The impecuniosity of the user will not necessarily absolve it from the duty to mitigate.

Exclusion Clauses

We have already considered the concept of concurrent liability where the possibility of contractual and tortious claims can arise from the same set of circumstances. This helps to explain why the exclusion and limitation of liability clauses that one typically finds in contracts often seek to exclude liability for the negligence of the provider.

We have already noted that the general attitude of the courts is to prohibit an action in tort where this avenue is being used merely to try to circumvent exclusions in a contract. Thus if the exclusion and limitation of liability clauses in a contract are effective to exclude or limit contractual liability, the chances of the party which has sustained the relevant damage succeeding in an action in tort are low. In this context, the reader is referred to the section on limitation and exclusion of contractual liability in Chapter 10.

Finally, it is worth noting that under the Unfair Contract Terms Act 1977, clauses which seek to exclude liability for death or personal injury caused by negligence are automatically invalid and those relating to the liability of a supplier for negligence where the customer suffers loss or damage other than death or personal injury are invalid to the extent that they are not reasonable.

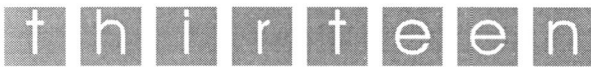

The Position and Duties of Directors

Personal liability of directors who fail to safeguard the interests of the company

INTRODUCTION

At the time of writing, there is much discussion as to the role of directors in the corporate environment centering on the report of the Hampel Committee on Corporate Governance and a Government Green Paper on company law. In addition to this, David Atkinson MP is still endeavouring to have 'The Companies (Millennium Computer Compliance) Bill 1997' enacted. It now seems very unlikely that this Bill will reach the statute books. If enacted, it would oblige companies to conduct an assessment of the capability of their key computer systems to deal with dates in the next Millennium and require directors to report on the action they propose to deal with potential problems.

These developments could lead to substantial changes in the field of company law and significantly alter the legal position of company directors significantly before the Year 2000.

However, at present, there is no specific Year 2000 legislation in the context of directors' duties or otherwise and this chapter will therefore assess the applicability of existing principles and duties to the Year 2000 situation.

Many companies will experience lesser or greater difficulties on account of the advent of the Year 2000. As we will see in this chapter, directors may be liable to certain persons for resultant losses in certain circumstances. Directors' conduct in the late 1990s may well be scrutinized in retrospect. In many cases, directors will have had to make decisions on difficult Year 2000 related issues. These might include determining whether to persevere with software which is not compliant on the basis of reassurances from the supplier that it would make it compliant pre-2000. Directors will also have to decide what steps and expenses are to be incurred in the context of contingency planning to cover the potential failure of systems or suppliers at the turn of the century.

Directors who are conscious of their duties and fear the mantle of the scapegoat should endeavour to keep detailed records of the reasons for their decisions. Such a record may well enable them to demonstrate that those decisions were made in fulfilment not dereliction of their duties.

Readers will doubtless be aware of the increasing tendency of companies to have non-executive directors. In relation to the Year 2000, non-executive directors may find themselves in a rather invidious position. Despite the fact that non-executive directors are not generally involved in the daily affairs of the company, English law does not fundamentally distinguish between the duties and liabilities of non-executive and executive directors. Whilst there are exceptions, the basic rule is that each individual director, whether executive or not, is equally liable for decisions of the board and that all directors are jointly and severally liable for breach of duty. In the Year 2000 context, the responsibilities of non-executive directors would seem to be twofold. First, they would appear to share the liabilities and duties of executive directors, as discussed below. Secondly, they would seem obliged to monitor the fulfilment of those same duties by the executive directors in their endeavours (or lack of them) to achieve Year 2000 compliance.

THE DUTY TO ACT IN GOOD FAITH IN THE COMPANY'S BEST INTERESTS

Directors must act in what they in good faith consider to be the company's best interests. Whilst this test is fundamentally subjective, it is tempered by objectivity to the extent that the actions or omissions of the director must be within the gamut of what a court determines a reasonable director could have considered to be in the company's interests. To fulfil this duty, it has been established that, amongst other things, a director must avoid situations where he finds himself with a conflict of interest. Let us in this context consider the example of a director of Company A who convinced the board in 1997 to buy PCs from Company B, a company in which he had a shareholding. In 1999, the director is told by the MD of Company B that the PCs are not Year 2000 compliant and that the cost of making them compliant would severely dent Company B's finances. The conflict for the director is clear.

THE DUTY TO ACT WITH CARE, SKILL AND DILIGENCE

Traditionally, this has not been a particularly onerous duty. In general terms, it was acceptable that a director delegated duties to appropriate persons, that he dedicated only a limited amount of his time to the company's affairs and that he acted in a manner consistent with what could be reasonably be expected from someone with his level of knowledge and experience.

This duty has over the course of time been evolving into a more onerous and objective one. It would seem that a director is now obliged to acquaint himself more fully with the company's overall situation and that the subjective test applied to his level of skill is tempered by an objective one in relation to the diligence which he exercises in relation to the company's matters. Furthermore, it would appear that in assessing whether a director has acted diligently, a court is likely to use as a benchmark what it considers that an ordinary man might have been expected to do in relation to his private interests.

This duty is likely to prove very relevant to the Year 2000 scenario. It might be applicable in many regards, including the steps taken in determining whom to appoint to fix Year 2000 bugs, the monitoring of employees entrusted with responsibility for the company's Year 2000 project and the establishment of appropriate contingency plans should the Millennium change adversely affect the company.

As the Year 2000 problem is essentially a technical one relating to the operation of software and hardware, it would seem very likely that the subjective skill criterion will result in IT directors being more harshly assessed than their less technically orientated brethren.

THE DUTY TO PAY HEED TO EMPLOYEES' INTERESTS

In addressing the Year 2000 or any other issue, directors are obliged to consider the interests of the company's employees. Actions or omissions which fail to contain or even exacerbate a company's exposure to the Year 2000 may ultimately result in the loss of jobs. Unfortunately, from the point of view of employees, this duty is owed to the company not the employees.

DIRECTORS IN DERELICTION OF DUTY – THE SANCTIONS

We have already seen that directors are bound by certain duties which could be significant in the context of Year 2000. We shall now consider what might happen to a director who fails to perform such duties adequately or at all. Before considering these, it is worth noting that a director may be able to escape liability to the company/shareholders if he can convince a court that he has acted 'reasonably and honestly' in all the circumstances.

Removal from Office

This is a power that the shareholders can exercise at a general meeting of a company by way of ordinary resolution.

In private companies, shareholders' freedom of exercise of this power may effectively be limited either legally if the Articles of Association accord weighted voting rights to shares held by directors or commercially if the directors' service contracts provide for substantial compensation on early termination. In public companies, endeavours by directors to entrench themselves legally would fall under the scrutiny and overriding control of The Stock Exchange.

Before resorting to such a measure, the shareholders would have to consider carefully whether such removal might give rise to claims for wrongful or unfair dismissal. Where the director is also an employee, the shareholders should ensure that they follow the company's disciplinary procedures and take into account any relevant terms in a service contract.

Action for Breach of Duty of Good Faith or Duty of Care, Skill and Diligence

The shareholders can make the decision on behalf of the company to sue the directors for financial recompense for breach of their duties. The rights of minority shareholders to obtain relief are limited. Typically, a minority shareholder would have to establish that it had been unfairly prejudiced by the directors' conduct of the company and in order to do so, would have to prove that there had been serious mismanagement of company affairs by the directors in question.

Action in Tort for Negligence

The fact that a director has been negligent in failing to address the Year 2000 situation adequately does not necessarily mean that he is in breach of duty. In such circumstances, the only option of aggrieved shareholders might be to sue the director(s) in damages for negligence.

Disqualification

If a company enters liquidation as a result of Year 2000-related problems which have been brought about by breach of duty by a director, then that director could face a disqualification order of between two and fifteen years. The culpability of the director will be relevant to whether and for how long such an order is made. If we plot a chart of the sorts of breaches likely to result in such an order, we might find the intentional suppression of information necessary for the company to become Year 2000 compliant at one end and an omission to provide the same information arising out of amnesia at the other. In cases of negligence or incompetence, it is likely to be a matter of degree.

RELIEF AGAINST THE CONSEQUENCES OF DERELICTION OF DUTY

Shareholder Ratification

The shareholders of a company have the power by a majority vote at a general meeting to ratify certain breaches of duty by a director. This power is only effective whilst the company is a going concern and the shareholders are in full possession of the relevant facts. Furthermore, it would not seem to be exercisable where the breach has involved dishonesty or illegality.

Insurance

Directors cannot be exempted from breach of duty by contractual provisions or the terms of a company's Articles of Association. However, many companies now indemnify their directors in respect of civil liability by effecting 'Directors and Officers' insurance policies to cover breaches of the sorts of duty we have discussed above. Obviously, the question as to whether any particular policy would cover a breach of duty in the context of Year 2000 would depend on the wording of the policy and the nature of the breach.

CORPORATE MANSLAUGHTER

Where the acts or omissions of a company are such as to cause the death of an individual, the courts will look behind the corporate veil to see whether the relevant act or omission could properly be attributed to one or more individuals running the company. Obviously, the smaller the company, the more likely it is that such identification will be possible.

We have to date had only one case of corporate manslaughter in this country where the managing director of a company was sent to prison because the gross negligence of the company which led to a death could be specifically attributed to that director.

At the time of writing, it is not possible to predict whether the Year 2000 will really lead to many or any deaths. However, it is clear that the effect of the Year 2000 on a whole host of mission critical software and embedded chip-containing machinery could cause personal injury or even death. Commonly cited examples include the failure of dialysis machines, air traffic control systems and the software controlling nuclear plants.

The Annual Audit

What will your auditors do if they find that the Year 2000 might threaten your commercial survival?

INTRODUCTION

Whilst our aim in this part of the book is to address the legal issues raised by the Year 2000, most readers will be considering the legal and technical issues raised by the Year 2000 from what is essentially a commercial perspective. One of the most important elements in the commercial life of a company is the annual visit of the auditor. If the auditor is unhappy with a company's accounts, this can have very serious consequences for a company. We therefore concluded that it would be useful to refer to the potential impact of the Year 2000 on the annual audit.

Many readers will be familiar with the auditor's annual visit. One of the auditor's duties is to identify any material misstatement in the company's accounts. Whilst there is no part of the audit process which is specifically Year 2000 orientated, the Year 2000 could materially impact on the auditor's assessment of the company's accounts.

In order to give a company a clean bill of health, the auditor must be convinced that the accounts present a 'true and fair' view of the company's financial position and the company's ability to continue as a 'going concern'. In certain circumstances, the unwillingness, lack of readiness or inability of a company to address the full implications of the Year 2000 may cause the auditor to lack this conviction.

In assessing the adequacy of a company's approach to the Year 2000 issue, the auditor is likely to consider to what extent the company is following what appears to be best practice in this area. A standard approach would typically include the appointment of a Year 2000 project manager, a detailed technical audit of the risks facing the company, the allocation of an adequate budget and contingency planning to address the company's areas of potential exposure.

If the auditor is not satisfied, he has various options, the most radical of which is the qualification of a company's accounts. The options are considered in more detail below. In the event of a company's accounts being qualified, the ability of that company to raise finance and, generally, to continue to trade may be severely impaired.

ACCURACY OF ACCOUNTS

There are various ways in which the Year 2000 could render accounts inaccurate. We set out some examples below:

- if the software used by a company to prepare its accounts is not Year 2000 compliant and as a result of this, it produces incorrect data, the company's accounts may be inaccurate and therefore not represent a 'true and fair' view of its financial status
- if equipment on which the company depends is not Year 2000 compliant and will either have to be made

compliant or shelved, the equipment should be written down and costs of adaptation or replacement should be factored into the company's financial statements
- if the company is likely to be sued on account of products which it has supplied not being Year 2000 compliant or for other reasons connected with the impact of Year 2000, then the potential costs involved should be factored into the accounts as a contingent liability.

GOING CONCERN

There are various ways in which the Year 2000 could impact on a company's ability to continue to trade. We set out some hypothetical examples below:

- the company has insufficient money to cover the necessary preventative or remedial work to ensure survival and continuity of its key IT systems
- the company whilst having the necessary resources to resolve the problems which it faces in the Year 2000 is unwilling to dedicate the necessary funds to achieve this
- the machinery on which the company depends contains non-compliant embedded chips and no plans have been or are being made to address this problem
- one or more of the company's key business partners are likely to let the company down on account of their own non-compliance.

If the auditor is not convinced that the directors have the situation under control or will be able and willing to take the necessary steps in time to nullify the potential problems, he may doubt whether the business will be able to continue as a going concern.

AUDITOR'S REPORT

We have considered above the sort of factors that might lead to an auditor being dissatisfied by what he discovers during the audit. If this is the case, he has various options. He may state that proper accounting records have not been kept. Most alarming for a company would be a qualification of its accounts either due to material misstatements of account balances or doubt as to its ability to continue as a going concern.

This danger was recently underlined in the context of Year 2000 by the Institute of Chartered Accountants in England and Wales. In October 1997, the ICAEW issued a warning to finance directors to the effect that the accounts of a company might be qualified if it failed to satisfy its auditors that its accounts properly reflected the potential impact of the Year 2000 on the company's business.

THE EFFECTS OF QUALIFICATION

If a company's accounts are qualified for the reasons set out in this chapter, this is likely to have severe effects on the company's financial health. Some of the potential effects are set out below:

- its ability to raise finance would be reduced as it would represent a worse risk in the eyes of potential lenders
- if it can raise finance, the costs involved would be increased as higher risk lending means higher interest rates
- if it is a public company, its share price is likely to be adversely affected as investors, becoming nervous, may sell and potential investors may be deterred.

Ironically, the negative effect on a company's financial

standing engendered by the qualification of its accounts may in itself prejudice a company's ability to raise the finances necessary to address its exposure to the effects of the advent of the Year 2000.

This leaves auditors in an unenviable 'Catch 22' position. If they fail to reflect a company's exposure to the Year 2000 in their audit report, this might constitute a breach of their duty to shareholders. However, qualification of a company's accounts which is either premature or results from an unduly negative assessment of the company's position in relation to the Year 2000 might exacerbate the company's position or even diminish its chances of survival.

Due Diligence

Mergers and Acquisitions – Should you take the Year 2000 risk?

INTRODUCTION

We have all heard of the 'black holes' that emerge in certain company's accounts after they have floated on the stock market or been taken over. This is perhaps the most alarming but certainly not the only unpleasant discovery that can come to light after a take-over has been completed. Facts such as these may with the benefit of hindsight make the purchase price that was paid seem excessively high or, at worst, render the whole take-over an awful mistake from the point of view of the acquirer.

Due diligence is the pre-contractual investigative process which potential acquirers instigate in order to try to avoid such nasty post-completion surprises.

Throughout this chapter we refer to take-overs and acquirers. However, we wish to make it clear that due diligence is a highly advisable, and indeed, invaluable exercise in the context of many different types of commercial transactions. For example, the contemplated transaction might be the partial or total acquisition or an entity of some or all of its assets, a loan by one company to another or a joint venture.

In the world today, the infrastructure of the vast majority of commercial entities relies heavily on either IT systems or industrial plant or a combination of the two.

The advent of Year 2000 poses various potential threats to the performance and even continuity of such infrastructures. This, in turn, may greatly reduce the intrinsic value of affected companies or even render them worthless.

Any entity which is considering launching a take-over bid for or even taking a stake in another should ensure that its due diligence exercise thoroughly examines the potential problems that the 'target' could encounter on account of the all important date change with which we are here concerned.

EXPOSURE OF THE TARGET TO THE YEAR 2000

In the analysis of the target's exposure, one must remember that Year 2000 problems might not necessarily arise in relation to events and the supplies of goods and services which will occur between the time of the transaction and the Year 2000. Such problems might also arise in relation to past supplies and events which in one way or another involved the target.

Let us move from the abstract to the concrete in suggesting some examples of how the Year 2000 might adversely affect a target company and raising certain associated questions. These are not set out in any particular order:

- the target has stored all its customer records in a database using a database program which crashes in January 2000 erasing all the records
- the target is wholly dependent on a monopolist for the

regular supply of a certain raw material. The monopolistic entity depends on machinery which contains Year 2000 non-compliant embedded chips. As a result of this, the supplier cannot supply the target and the target cannot service its own customers' requirements whose own businesses are consequentially adversely affected. This puts the target in breach of contract with various customers, which not only destroys much customer goodwill but also exposes it to potentially crippling litigation

- the target business consists of the manufacture and maintenance of lifts. Under the terms of its maintenance contracts, it guarantees that any problem with the operation of the lifts will be fixed within 24 hours. Certain of the lifts maintained by the company contain non-compliant embedded chips which cause the lifts to break down. The replacement of the chips is, to say the least, a very complicated time-consuming job which will take several months to carry out. The breakdown of the lifts may also cause the target to be in breach of the implied warranties regarding fitness for purpose and/or satisfactory quality examined in Chapter 10 in the context of contract law
- the target may derive a great proportion of its turnover from one or two customers whose own businesses may fail because of Year 2000 non-compliance
- the target appointed a facilities manager in 1995 to run its data processing operations on a ten-year contract. In 1997 the facilities manager becomes aware of the Year 2000 issue and in 1998 it checks its contract with the target and finds that its obligations would include the rectification of non-compliant software. The facilities manager does not want to jeopardise its revenue stream but determines that it would lose a lot of money if it had to make the software compliant. The

manager therefore invokes a 6 months' termination clause under the contract in May 1999, leaving the target in a potentially ruinous lurch in November 1999
- has the target in the past sold off assets or even parts of its operations in respect of which it has continuing liabilities which might be triggered by the advent of the Year 2000?
- if the target could potentially lay off its own exposure to Year 2000 on other entities, would this ability be adversely affected by the fact or form of the takeover?
- if the target has engaged the services of a Year 2000 solution provider, would that solution provider be contractually liable in the event of non-compliance and, if so, is it likely that the solution provider would be able to pay damages should a claim be successful?
- has the target carried out either a technical and/or contractual audit of its exposure to Year 2000 (as discussed in Chapter 9 above)? If so, how thorough were such audits, what exposure did they reveal and what steps have been taken to address such exposure?
- does the target have relevant insurance cover against its exposure and would such cover be affected by the takeover?

These are but a few examples of how a target might be directly or indirectly affected by the Year 2000. Hopefully, from this it can be seen that potential acquirers or investors would be ill advised not to scrutinize the overall context in which a target operates and that this investigation should amongst other things extend to an assessment of the Year 2000 exposure of the target to its key customers and from its key suppliers. Indeed, the due diligence exercise should, amongst many other things, comprise a Year 2000 contractual audit in respect of the target of the type suggested in Chapter 9.

If the due diligence exercise reveals that the target may well be adversely affected by the advent of the Year 2000, the next question is whether the problem can be remedied and, if so, how easily and at what cost?

Another fundamental issue which falls for consideration in the valuation and analysis of the viability of the business of a target is whether the target could reduce or even eliminate its potential exposure by making successful claims against other entities with whom it has contractual relationships, under which the exposure in question is covered by the obligations or liability of the other party to the contract.

HOW TO ADDRESS PROBLEMS REVEALED BY THE DUE DILIGENCE EXERCISE

In the event that the due diligence exercise reveals substantial exposure of the target to the Year 2000, there are various approaches and measures which the potential acquirer may follow or take. We set out some of these below:

- abandon the proposed transaction altogether
- renegotiate the price
- alter the structure of the proposed transaction from a purchase of shares to a purchase of assets in order to try to avoid the contractual liabilities of the target
- secure third party guarantees to cover its exposure
- insist on appropriate express warranties and/or indemnities being inserted into the contract which is to govern the proposed transaction
- defer the payment of all or a part of the acquisition price until such time as it can be determined whether the value of the target will be adversely affected
- take out appropriate insurance to cover product liability, legal costs or other risks

- delay the transaction until such time as it can be determined whether the value of the target will be adversely affected.

Data Protection

Could the Year 2000 cause you to infringe the laws relating to personal data?

The Data Protection Act 1984 seeks to protect individuals against misuse of personal information relating to them, particularly if it is inaccurate.

First, we will consider the principles which form the infrastructure of the data protection regime. We will then consider the relevance of the requirement of registration under the Act in the context of the Year 2000 and the potentially thorny issue of the export of data to other jurisdictions.

THE PRINCIPLES

The fulcrum of the Act consists of eight principles of data protection. These set out the standards which data users should observe when processing personal data concerning living individuals. The first principle stipulates that personal data shall be processed fairly. The fifth principle requires that all data 'shall be accurate and, where necessary, kept up to date'. The eighth principle obliges data users to implement 'appropriate security measures' against 'unauthorised access to, or alteration, disclosure or destruction of personal data and against accidental loss or destruction of personal data'.

There is substantial potential for widespread corruption of personal data as a direct or indirect result of the effects produced by the advent of the Year 2000 and dates such as 29th February, 2000 on the performance of software and hardware. Each of the three data protection principles cited above could be infringed by such corruption.

In relation to the first principle, data regarding the age of data subjects could be corrupted, prejudicing their entitlements or prospects in one way or another. In the context of the fifth principle, it is clear that inaccurate data would result from such corruption.

In the context of the eighth principle, the question arises as to what would constitute 'appropriate security measures' in relation to the dangers presented by the Year 2000. Every allegation that the eighth principle has been breached will have to be assessed individually in the light of its circumstances. However, in each case, the key factors are likely to include whether the data user had implemented a comprehensive Year 2000 project, comprising elements such as risk assessment, impact analysis, remedial and curative action.

REGISTRATION

It is now common practice for IT users to engage the services of external service providers to render part or the whole of their operations Year 2000 compliant. The solution provider will often have access to data which is covered by the 1984 Act. In such circumstances, the data user should ensure that its registration under the Act covers the provision of the data to a third party such as the solution provider.

In addition, the activities of the solution provider itself may necessitate its registration under the Act.

EXPORT OF DATA

An important part of the role of data protection legislation is to prevent the export of data to jurisdictions where there is no equivalent system of protection. This has become of even greater significance by virtue of the Second Data Protection Directive, which must be implemented by European Union member states by October 1998. The UK is doing this by primary legislation, which will give rise to a new Data Protection Act. We will briefly consider the current position and the forthcoming regime.

Current Position

It is fair to say that the current position is unclear and there are a number of issues which are yet to be resolved with regard to the export of data. Under the 1984 Act, a data user may register an intention to export data world-wide. This will remain the case until the new Act. Although the Registrar has the power to prevent export of data by use of a Transfer Prohibition Notice, this power has been exercised only once.

The New Regime

The approach of the new Act will be that data must not be exported unless the jurisdiction to which the data is to be sent has in force an adequate level of protection. The aim is that within the EU there will be free exchange of data as all member countries will implement the Directive and therefore have the necessary level of protection.

The problem will arise in relation to exports of data from the EU. At the time of writing, there is much discussion as to the establishment of a 'black list' of jurisdictions where the level of protection is deemed inadequate. The assessment of adequacy will be based on two requirements. The first is that there should be a substantive provision of law in the relevant jurisdiction guaranteeing an adequate level of protection. The second is a procedural requirement that there be a data protection registrar or equivalent functionary in place.

The United States poses a particular problem as the data protection regimes differs from state to state. Where a state has privacy laws in place, this is likely to meet the first requirement but this, of course, does not help with the second criterion.

There is a provision in the Directive that data can be exported to a 'black-listed' jurisdiction if protection is afforded by contractual provision. The application of this exception is problematic in England and Wales because the doctrine of privity of contract will preclude the data user from having any right to enforce such contractual rights against a foreign recipient of data who is in breach of contract.

CONCLUSION

The necessity of ensuring compliance with data protection legislation in the context of trying to procure a Year 2000 solution may prove an unwelcome extra hurdle. It is likely that the observance of data protection legislation is not uppermost in the minds of those who are concerned to survive the advent of the Year 2000. In view of the fact that the provision of data to a foreign solution provider may well span both the current and new regimes, the problems are likely to be compounded.

Litigation and other forms of dispute resolution

How to recover your losses and enforce your remedies

INTRODUCTION

Besides litigation, we also consider other forms of dispute resolution mechanism, namely arbitration and alternative dispute resolution.

From the technical analysis earlier in this book (Part One), it seems clear that enormous losses will be suffered by many companies as a result of the technical problems which arise from the advent of the Year 2000. From a legal perspective it will of course be crucial to determine who should bear such losses. Obviously, in many cases there will be disagreements, particularly between users and suppliers but also between different entities in the supply chain as to where the liability for such losses should fall.

In the absence of amicable settlements, it will be necessary to turn to the existing forms of dispute resolution to resolve such matters. Indeed, at the time of writing there are already several cases in the offing in the United States regarding Year 2000 concerning the inability of PCs and tills to deal with the advent of the Year 2000 and the rights of software suppliers to charge for Year 2000 compliant upgrades.

We believe that the two most likely modes of resolution will be litigation and alternative dispute resolution ('ADR'). Arbitration is also a possibility. Both litigation and arbitration work on an adversarial basis. This means that there is a third party, either the judge or the arbitrator who hears the evidence and reaches a decision. Arbitration, like ADR but unlike litigation, depends on the parties' agreement to submit the dispute to that forum.

ADR differs from the other two types of resolution in that it is a form of mediation whereby a third party, the mediator, seeks to help the parties in dispute to reach a conciliatory consensus. The mediator cannot impose any decision on either party against its will. For this reason, we believe that it will be particularly suited to Year 2000 dispute determination. Moreover, the recent Woolf Report on Access to Justice favours an extension of ADR. We will therefore consider ADR first before turning to the two more traditional forms of dispute resolution.

As we anticipate that most claims in this area will pertain to software, we will refer to software in this chapter. However, in most instances, the points made will be equally applicable to non-compliant hardware or firmware.

ALTERNATIVE DISPUTE RESOLUTION

In the field of IT, many relationships are ongoing with many users depending on the provision of maintenance, facilities management, outsourcing and other services. In certain cases, there may be no more than one or a handful of potential service providers. In such circumstances, a victory won by a user in the adversarial context of litigation or arbitration may be pyrrhic, destroying the relationship or, at least, the goodwill on which the user is dependent.

The benefit of ADR in such a context is obvious. If the outcome is positive, the parties reach a compromise with which they are both content and if the outcome is negative, then, apart from the wasted costs, neither party is in a worse position than before ADR was tried.

The suitability of ADR in the Year 2000 context relates not only to its non-confrontational nature but also to the fact that it could enable pragmatic solutions which neither litigation nor arbitration could provide and which are what the user really needs. Most notably, such solutions could relate to co-operation in either the funding or methodology necessary to fix software which is not Year 2000 compliant.

Although the potential advantages of ADR are clear, we would temper our enthusiasm with a few notes of caution. First, the process of ADR can be abused by a supplier who has no intention of reaching a mediated settlement but hopes that by the time the user realizes this, it will be out of time to instigate court proceedings. Secondly, ADR usually results in the parties putting their cards on the table. This is fine if settlement is reached. However, if ADR is unsuccessful, the advantage which can be derived in litigation from cloaking one's hand will have been lost if the parties end up in court. Finally, ADR, if unsuccessful, will have produced nothing apart from wasted time and money.

LITIGATION

Jurisdiction

Cross-border deals represent a high proportion of world trade. In the world of software, it is common for the manufacturer or supplier to be based in one country but the user in another. In most cases, there will be a written licence relating to that transaction specifying the relevant jurisdiction and legal system which will govern any disputes between the parties. For example, it is extremely common for a user based in the UK to become a licensee of a software product originating in the US and, in respect of which, the licence provides that in the event of dispute, the governing law will be that of, eg California and the courts competent to hear such dispute will be those based in that state.

The issues of jurisdiction and applicable law are discussed to some degree in Chapter 10. However, they are very complicated and certainly not a focus of this book. We provide the example above in order to demonstrate that it will be far from clear in many cases that a UK based licensee of software who wants to sue in respect of a product which is not Year 2000 compliant will end up doing so either in the UK or on the basis of the laws of England.

Having exposed these potential difficulties, we will proceed with the rest of this discussion of Year 2000 litigation on the basis that the dispute in question is to be heard by a court in England or Wales and that English law will be applied.

Limitation Periods

It is vital to bear in mind that even if one has a cause of action against another entity for non-compliance or any other matter, one must bring that claim within the statutory limitation periods, six years in the case of an action based upon breach of contract. Thus a defendant will probably have an impregnable defence if a plaintiff starts an action outside of the time limits.

Trigger Dates

The starting point of the limitation period in Year 2000 actions has not been specifically determined by the courts of England and Wales. However, it seems clear that in respect of a claim based on a breach of contract, the limit is six years from the date of provision of the software. This means that anyone waiting to sue till Year 2000 will be out of time in respect of any software acquired before the relevant date in 1994. In the unlikely event that the reader has entered a relevant contract by deed, it should however note that a 12 year limit applies.

For an action in tort, where the allegation in the Year 2000 context is very likely to be negligence in supplying non-compliant software, the limitation period is also six years. However, in this case, the six years will probably be measured from the time of the damage being sustained which in most cases will be the time when the software 'malfunctions'. As in most cases such damage is unlikely to occur before the Year 2000, it can be clearly seen that most potential plaintiffs will have until 2006 to initiate such actions.

A plaintiff suing in negligence has an extra three years to initiate proceedings where the damage in question was latent. This supplementary period starts from the earliest date on which the plaintiff had not only the right to sue, but also knew, or reasonably could have known, about the damage and its attributability to the defendant's negligence. The relevance of this extra period is limited to circumstances where the three year period expires after the conventional six year period which runs from the accrual of the cause of action.

In any event, a longstop of 15 years applies to actions in negligence (other than for personal injury) and this could produce the final Year 2000 actions as late as 2015.

In the section below on 'Multiple Parties', we will consider the possibility of fault for Year 2000 non-compliance being shared by various parties. In that connection, in the event that damages are awarded against one of those parties, it may seek a contribution from one or more of the others. In order to allow time for such contributions to be sought, the law provides for an extended limitation period of two years from the date on which the initial defendant is established to be liable during which time the defendant can claim against the other(s).

This extended period operates irrespective of whether the matter in question is based on contract (including those under seal) or tort by making available a two year extension to any limitation period. However, if the initial defendant is established to be liable at a time when there remains at least two years of the ordinarily applicable limitation period, this additional limitation period will have no effect.

Holding back the years

If a plaintiff is facing the expiry of the relevant time limit, it will be sensible for it either to initiate an action before the time limit expires or to reach an agreement with the potential defendant to the effect that the sands of time are suspended. This is only possible if both the potential plaintiff and the potential defendant agree that time will not run against the plaintiff for the period that the 'standstill agreement' is in effect. This may be a means for the parties to avoid unnecessary litigation into which the potential plaintiff might otherwise have been forced for fear of becoming statute barred by reason of expiry of the limitation period. Although it is believed that such an agreement if properly drafted would be honoured by a court, there is at present no directly binding authority for this view and, to be completely safe, one should always issue proceedings in time.

As stated above, if faced by the limitation time pressures, the potential plaintiff should consider issuing a writ within the limitation period, even if it is expected or hoped that the dispute can ultimately be resolved by settlement without recourse to full-blown litigation. Indeed, in certain circumstances, the issue of such writs can actually facilitate settlement.

A holding writ is of only temporary value unless the plaintiff can back it up with a substantiated case. This is because a writ must be served on the potential defendant (unless it is resident outside England and Wales) within four months of its issue and if the writ is specious in that it does not reveal a proper case, the defendant can and often will successfully apply for it to be 'struck out'.

The writ will have to contain or be followed shortly by a statement of claim which is a court pleading setting out the plaintiff's case. In the normal course of events, this will be followed by other pleadings. The most significant of these is usually the defence which is sometimes coupled with a counterclaim against the plaintiff.

Multiple Parties

In many cases it may be difficult for a user to establish which part of its IT system is responsible for the problems which it experiences in Year 2000. A typical user's IT system may well comprise many different software and hardware elements all of which are to some extent intertwined and inter-dependent. In this context, one can be sure that there will be a lot of entities busily attempting to pass the buck either up or down the supply chain. It may well be that total liability cannot be laid at any one door and that there are several culprits, possibly including the user itself.

Such a convoluted scenario brings with it the likelihood of litigation involving a variety of causes of action and a multitude of different entities simultaneously denying their own liability and alleging that of other parties. In order to avoid a host of related but separate actions, the rules of court procedure provide amongst other things for a group of plaintiffs to sue a group of defendants, and for those defendants to sue one another, all in respect of the same losses.

Statute gives the right to any person liable in respect of any damage suffered by another to recover a contribution from any other person liable in respect of the same damage (whether jointly or otherwise) regardless of whether the liability is in tort or contract. In the Year 2000 context, it is quite conceivable that various parties might be liable in respect of the same non-compliance. Consider for example a piece of machinery which contains a non-compliant embedded chip. The machine breaks down in January 2000 and the user suffers losses. Those who might be liable include the manufacturer of the chip, that manufacturer's distributor who supplied the chip to the machine manufacturer, the machine manufacturer itself and its distributor who supplied the chip to the user.

The level of contributions payable by each party will be determined by the court on the basis of what is a fair reflection of that party's level of responsibility for the damage.

Where a court finds that the plaintiff and various entities involved in the supply chain are all culpable, the court can determine a judgement figure in favour of the plaintiff user, who can seek to recover this figure in full against any one of the defendants who are effectively made jointly and severally liable.

The courts can in certain circumstances also merge actions which were initiated separately or separate causes of action or parties which had previously been part of the same proceedings.

Representative actions are also possible where one or more members of a group with a common cause of action against a particular entity or entities represents all the others as well as itself.

Evidence

In both civil and criminal cases, the court or tribunal will apply the relevant law. However, the resolution of disputes is not an abstract legal matter. In determining liability, the court will have to establish whether on the basis of the facts in question, it is satisfied that the necessary proof has been presented to substantiate the claims or charges.

The general rule in relation to both claims and defences is that he who asserts must prove. Whereas in criminal cases, the plaintiff must prove its case beyond reasonable doubt, in civil cases, the requirement is to establish what is alleged on the 'balance of probabilities'.

A plaintiff who fails to prove his claim on the balance of probabilities will of course be in a worse position than he would have been in had he never litigated. The wasted costs brings to mind the old cliché 'throwing good money after bad'.

Hence, one should be very cautious before initiating proceedings. The assessment of whether to proceed must above all other things be based on the strength of one's evidence. If there is a good chance that in the eyes of the court, one's evidence would be insufficiently strong to acquit the applicable burden of evidence, then the decision to litigate would probably be a bad one.

There are many works which analyse the nature and quality of evidence. Suffice it to say for present purposes that anyone who has to make decisions on which not only their jobs but also the outcome of future litigation might depend would be well advised to make and keep accurate and contemporaneous written and/or audio records of the factors involved in the decision-making process. Where this involves suppliers' reassurances as to the ability of their products or companies to deal with the Year 2000, or more general continuity representations, the written or taped record should, if possible, be obtained on the supplier's letter head or of the supplier's voice.

Such records would typically include contracts with suppliers and service providers, fault logs, correspondence, telephone conversations and minutes of meetings as well as data back-ups. In taking a view as to the extent of necessary record-keeping, one should err on the side of caution and include any matter which might possibly be relevant.

Record-keeping will also be vital from the supplier's point of view. For example, if a customer alleges that it logged numerous fault calls with a supplier in relation to the performance of functionality of a software program, but the supplier's records do not reflect this, this may be crucial to the supplier's defence.

In most situations, it will be important to keep records of what was on the particular computer or network, its specifications, and its capabilities before it is altered by new products or by maintenance. A regularly updated disk or tape archive of the data held on a system will be useful in substantiating claims for lost data.

Expert Evidence

In areas of litigation where the determination of the factors of causation is complex, expert evidence is often crucial to the outcome. Year 2000 litigation is sure to necessitate the involvement of expert computer professionals. To be effective, an expert must be respected in his field and present his evidence both clearly and impartially.

Forcing the Issue

A litigant may be in a position to avail itself of various procedural stratagems in endeavouring to win its case without going the whole distance. Four of these are considered briefly below.

Summary Judgement

The rules of court provide for a party to apply for what is known as 'summary judgement'. To obtain this, the plaintiff must convince the court that there is no real defence to the claim. If the applicant is successful, it will obtain judgement without having to go through all the normal procedural steps and laying out the associated costs involved in litigation.

Order for Security for Costs

A defendant may in certain circumstances be able to take advantage of a plaintiff's lack of funds by convincing a court to make an order for security for costs against the plaintiff. For such an application to succeed, the court needs to assess various factors, including the strength of the plaintiff's case and to be satisfied that if the plaintiff's claim were to fail, it could not pay the defendant's costs.

Payment into Court

Another tactic which may be deployed by a defendant is to pay a sum into court. This sum will be less than that claimed by the plaintiff but should be pitched at around the level of damages which the plaintiff might recover if things do not go too well for it. If the plaintiff does not accept the payment, the case proceeds to trial, and the plaintiff wins but is awarded damages which do not exceed the sum paid in, then the plaintiff will be liable not only for its own costs but also those of the defendant from the time that the payment-in was made.

Calderbank Letter

Faced with Year 2000 litigation in which the plaintiff demands particular action on the part of the defendant, the defendant might bring similar pressure to bear on the plaintiff by writing a 'Calderbank letter'. In such a letter, the defendant would offer to take limited steps along the path set out in the statement of claim.

ARBITRATION

Although we have already indicated that we do not consider that this will be the principal methodology adopted to resolve Year 2000 disputes, we will make a few brief points as to the nature of arbitration, its advantages and disadvantages.

Whereas the arbitral procedure and rules of evidence are often based on those found in litigation, the parties are free to agree on other modes. This means that arbitration may in certain cases be far less formalistic and expensive than litigation. In the context of Year 2000 where, as has already been intimated, the dispute may be highly technical, it is particularly significant that the parties are able to appoint an arbitrator with particular expertise.

When contrasting arbitration with litigation, it should be noted that any cost savings achieved through the adoption of simplified rules of evidence and procedure may be more than set off by the additional costs of room hire and the fees of the arbitrator. The process may also be less efficient than litigation due to the more restricted range of powers of the arbitrator.

PRACTICAL GUIDANCE

If a user decides either before or after Year 2000 that it has a good claim against a supplier for non-compliant software, it should send the supplier a letter before action threatening imminent action if the supplier does not comply within a fixed period with the user's demands as set out in that letter. The demands will probably centre either on the supplier making the software compliant or agreeing to reimburse the user in respect of costs incurred in getting a third party to do so.

If the user's demands are not met within the time limit set out in the letter before action, it should issue a writ and serve it on the defendant (as set out above in relation to holding writs).

BSI Year 2000 Compliance definition and associated documentation

Note. The contents of this appendix are provided by way of illustration and information only. No responsibility is accepted for their use. Detailed legal advice from suitably qualified lawyers should be obtained before use or adaptation of any part hereof. What follows is a reproduction of British Standards Institution document number ISBN 0 580 29746 2. The attention of readers is drawn to the conditions included therein under which it may be further copied.

APPENDIX A

A DEFINITION OF **YEAR 2000** CONFORMITY REQUIREMENTS

Introduction

This document addresses what is commonly known as Year 2000 conformity (also sometimes known as century or millennium compliance). It provides a definition of this expression and requirements that must be satisfied in equipment and products which use dates and times.

It has been prepared by British Standards Institution committee BDD/I/-/3 in response to demand from UK industry, commerce and the public sector. It is the result of work from the following bodies whose contributions are gratefully acknowledged: BT, Cap Gemini, CCTA, Coopers & Lybrand, Halberstam Elias, ICL, National Health Service, National Westminster Bank.

BSI-DISC would also like to thank the following organizations for their support and encouragement in the development of this definition: Taskforce 2000, Barclays Bank, British Airways, Cambridgeshire County Council, Computer Software Services Association, Department of Health, Ernst & Young, Federation of Small Businesses, IBM, ICI, National Power, Paymaster Agency, Prudential Assurance, Reuters, Tesco Stores.

While every care has been taken in developing this document, the contributing organizations accept no liability for any loss or damage caused, arising directly or indirectly, in connection with reliance on its contents except to the extent that such liability may not be excluded at law. Independent legal advice should be sought by any person or organization intending to enter into a contractual commitment relating to Year 2000 conformity requirements.

This entire document or the definition section may be freely copied provided that the text is reproduced in full, the source acknowledged and the reference number of the document is quoted.

THE DEFINITION

Year 2000 conformity shall mean that neither performance nor functionality is affected by dates prior to, during and after the year 2000.

In particular:
Rule 1. No value for current date will cause any interruption in operation.

Rule 2. Date-based functionality must behave consistently for dates prior to, during and after year 2000.

Rule 3. In all interfaces and data storage, the century in any date must be specified either explicitly or by unambiguous algorithms or inferencing rules.

Rules 4. Year 2000 must be recognized as a leap year.

AMPLIFICATION OF THE DEFINITION AND RULES
General Explanation

Problems can arise from some means of representing dates in computer equipment and products and from date-logic embedded in purchased goods or services, as the year 2000 approaches and during and after that year. As a result, equipment or products, including embedded control logic, may fail completely, malfunction or cause data to be corrupted.

To avoid such problems, organizations must check, and modify if necessary, internally produced equipment and products and similarly check externally supplied equipment and products with their suppliers. The purpose of this document is to allow such checks to be made on a basis of common understanding.

Where checks are made with external suppliers, care should be taken to distinguish between claims of conformity and the ability to demonstrate conformity.

Rule 1

1.1 This rule is sometimes known as *general integrity*.

1.2 If this requirement is satisfied, roll-over between all significant time demarcations (e.g. days, months, years, centuries) will be performed correctly.

1.3 *Current date* means today's date as known to the equipment or product.

Rule 2

2.1 This rule is sometimes known as *date integrity*.

2.2 This rule means that all equipment and products must calculate, manipulate and represent dates correctly for the purposes for which they were intended.

2.3 The meaning of *functionality* includes both processes and the results of those processes.

2.4 If desired, a reference point for date values and calculations may be added by organizations; e.g. as defined by the Gregorian calendar.

2.5 No equipment or product shall use particular date values for special meanings; e.g. "99" to signify "no end value" or "end of file" or "00" to mean "not applicable" or "beginning of file".

Rule 3
3.1 This rule is sometimes known as *explicit/implicit century*.
3.2 It covers two general approaches:
   (a) explicit representation of the year in dates: e.g. by using four digits or by including a century indicator. In this case, a reference may be inserted (e.g. 4-digit years as allowed by ISO stanadard 8601:1988) and it may be necessary to allow for exceptions where domain-specific standards (e.g. standards relating to Electronic Data Interchange, Automatic Teller Machines or Bankers Automated Clearing Services) should have precedence.
   (b) the use of inferencing rules: e.g. two-digit years with a value greater than 50 imply 19xx, those with a value equal to or less than 50 imply 20xx. Rules for century inferencing as a whole must apply to all contexts in which the date is used, although different inferencing rules may apply to different date sets.

General Notes
For Rules 1 and 2 in particular, organizations may wish to specify allowable ranges for values of current date and dates to be manipulated. The ranges may relate to one or more of the feasible life-span of equipment or products or the span of dates required to be represented by the organization's business processes. Tests for specifically critical dates may also be added (e.g. for leap years, end of year, etc). Organizations may wish to append additional material in support of local requirements.

Where the term century is used, clear distinction should be made between the "value" denoting the century (e.g. 20th) and its representation in dates (e.g. 19xx); similarly, 21st and 20xx.

Model Year 2000 Software Compliance Questionnaire

Note. The contents of this appendix are provided by way of illustration and information only. No responsibility is accepted for their use. Detailed legal advice from suitably qualified lawyers should be obtained before use or adaptation of any part hereof.

APPENDIX B

[Pro Forma] covering letter

Dear [   ],

Product Questionnaire – Year 2000 and Third Millennium Compliance

Please complete a copy of the questionnaire enclosed in respect of each of the separate product versions which we are currently using or intending to use.

The information supplied will enable us to assess the suitability of your software or hardware for our continuing business operations.

Please review the defined terms on the following page(s) before completing the questionnaire.

Please note that all your replies will be kept on our records for the purposes of checking Year 2000 and Third Millennium compliance of your products and services.

Yours sincerely

Defined Terms

In the questionnaire, the following terms have the following meanings:

Product: the application or hardware and version number to be inserted at the top of each questionnaire.

Compliant: neither product performance nor functionality being affected by any date change caused by the advent of the year 2000 or any other date.

Corrective Release: a subsequent product version which is compliant.

Date: information representing any particular point in time, by reference to year, month and day of the month.

PTF: Program temporary fix.

Source Code: the product in human readable form sufficient to enable a programmer to amend and recompile the product.

Model Compliance Questionnaire

Product:_____

Version:_____

IF THE ANSWERS TO QUESTIONS 1–8 ARE ALL YES, TICK HERE ☐

AND THEN ANSWER QUESTION 9.
IF NOT, PLEASE ANSWER ALL THE QUESTIONS.

1. Is the Product Compliant?
   Yes/No

2. Does the Product accept two digit year input?
   Yes/No

3. If the answer to question 2 is yes, does the Product automatically convert two year digit entries to include the current century and millennium?
   Yes/No

4. If the answer to question 2 is yes, are years processed and output as four digits?
   Yes/No

5. At all documented external interfaces does the Product accept and provide only valid 4-digit Dates?
   Yes/No

6. Does the Product correctly distinguish between Dates from different centuries and millennia?
   Yes/No

7. Does the Product correctly perform calculations involving Dates from or spanning different centuries or millennia?
   Yes/No

APPENDIX B

8. If Dates are currently stored without century indications, can they be amended and processed thereafter without alteration to the Source Code?
   Yes/No

9. If the answer to question 8 is yes, please explain how:

10. If the answer to question 8 is no, are you willing to make the Source Code available to us?
    Yes/No

11. If the answer to question 10 is yes, please indicate on what basis:

12. Please detail any specific hardware functionality, eg specific microprocessor routines, on which the Product relies:

IF THE ANSWER TO ANY OF QUESTIONS 1–8 IS NO, BUT THERE IS OR WILL BE A CORRECTIVE RELEASE WHICH IS COMPLIANT AND IN RESPECT OF WHICH ALL THE ANSWERS TO QUESTIONS 1–8 WOULD BE YES, PLEASE PROVIDE THE INFORMATION REQUESTED AT QUESTIONS 13–18.

13. Version number of Corrective Release or PTF level:

14. When will Corrective Release or PTF be available?

15. Please confirm that the Corrective Release or PTF is included under the maintenance agreement.
    Yes/No

16. Will data from the Product be readable by the Corrective Release in native format and without further processing by us?
    Yes/No

17. Does the Corrective Release retain all the other functionality of the Product?
    Yes/No

18. Will you make available any facilities to us to assist in migration from the Product to the Corrective Release?
Yes/No

REGARDLESS OF ANY OF THE ANSWERS GIVEN ABOVE, PLEASE ANSWER THE FOLLOWING QUESTIONS:

19. Will you ensure that the Product remains compatible with standard interface products such as BACS, SWIFT, etc?
Yes/No

20. Will you offer any facilities for us to test their interfaces to the Compliant versions of the Product in an environment that is able to simulate post-1999 dates?
Yes/No

21. Will you enable us throughout the licence period to test the Product using post-1999 dates without adversely impacting on our ability to use the Product?
Yes/No

Model Request for Year 2000 Compliance statement and warranty to be sent to suppliers

Note. The contents of this appendix are provided by way of illustration and information only. No responsibility is accepted for their use. Detailed legal advice from suitably qualified lawyers should be obtained before use or adaptation of any part hereof.

APPENDIX C

[PRO FORMA] COVERING LETTER

Dear [   ],

Year 2000 and Third Millennium Compliance

As you are aware, there is much concern as to the ability of software and hardware systems to cope with the millennium date change.

We are in the process of evaluating our own situation. As an extension of this evaluation, we wish to ensure that your ability to supply us with goods and services will be unaffected by the date change from 1999 to 2000 and all other date changes, including without limitation 29th February 2000.

Please have somebody with appropriate authority sign and return the attached compliance statement and warranty. This information will confirm to us your continuing ability to meet our requirements.

Yours sincerely

MODEL YEAR 2000 COMPLIANCE STATEMENT AND WARRANTY

We, the undersigned, hereby represent and warrant to [   ] that our ability to supply goods and services to [   ] will be unaffected by the date change from 1999 to 2000 and all other date changes, including without limitation 29th February 2000. We understand that in making future orders from us, [   ] will be relying on this representation and warranty.

Signed   ....

Position/title of Signatory ....

For and on behalf of   ....(Supplier's name)

Date

Model Year 2000 Compliance warranty

Note. The contents of this appendix are provided by way of illustration and information only. No responsibility is accepted for their use. Detailed legal advice from suitably qualified lawyers should be obtained before use or adaptation of any part hereof.

NB. When using this warranty or part thereof within a contract, you must adapt the wording to fit in with the contract in question. For example if the term 'Licensor' is not used in the contract, then the term which is used, eg 'Supplier' must be adopted instead. Additionally, the wording in the warranty should be adapted to reflect the nature of the product in question. Before you adapt the warranty in any way, you should seek legal advice as to the implications of such adaptation.

APPENDIX D

Year 2000 Compliance Warranty

The Licensor represents and warrants that:-

1. No error or interruption in the operation of the [software/product] will result directly or indirectly from the passage from the twentieth century to the twenty-first century or from the extra day occurring in any leap year in the twentieth or twenty-first century or from the occurrence of any other date;
2. No reduction or alteration in the functionality of the [software/product] will result directly or indirectly from the passage from the twentieth century to the twenty-first century or from the extra day occurring in any leap year in the twentieth or twenty-first century or from the occurrence of any other date;
3. The [software/product] will not process any data which includes a date which does not specify the century;
4. All date related output and results produced by the [software/product] shall include an indication of the century;
5. The [software/product] will produce accurate results in respect of calculations and other data processing which span the twentieth and twenty-first centuries; and
6. Interfaces and reporting facilities comprised by the [software/product] will support four digit year processing;

Indemnity

To the extent that the Licensor fails in any respect to comply with the Year 2000 compliance warranty, the Licensor agrees to indemnify and hold fully harmless the Licensee against any loss, damage or expense sustained or incurred directly or indirectly as a result of such failure.

Index

acceptance tests   35, 86
accounts *see* company accounts
application programs   7, 51, 56, 67, 68
applications software   49–50
arbitration *see* dispute resolution
Articles of Association   159, 161
Atkinson, David   155
audit *see* company accounts
auditors   163–4
awareness raising   10–13, 17, 59, 72

'battle of the forms'   79, 108
BIOS   27, 45, 48
bi-partite analysis   77–8
   see also contract law
British Standards Institution (BSI)   xi, 85, 102
   compliance definition 191–4
BT (British Telecom)   100

change management   65–7
'Clapham Omnibus' principle   113
CMOS   46
communication   37–8, 59
Companies (Millennium Computer Compliance) Bill   155
company accounts
   annual audit   163–7
   auditor's report   166
   effects of qualification   166–7
company law   155
compliance xi,   43, 53–4
   investigation   43–52, 63
   non-compliance   54–9
   statements   48

techniques   53, 57
testing   67–9
   see also 'Year 2000 compliance'
consultancy   62–4
consumer
   legal definition   122–4
Consumer Protection Act (1987)   150, 151, 152
contingency plans   29, 30–31
contract law   75–104, 105–29, 131–9
   agreements   71–2
   ambiguity   129
   applicability   107–8, 182
   bipartite analysis   71–2, 84, 90–92, 94
   consideration   109–10, 146
   copyright   78, 87, 123
   damages   132, 133–8, 183
   disclaimers   80–81
   duty   147
   'entire agreement clause'   106–7, 110, 133
   estoppel   107, 128
   exclusion clauses   154
   facilities management   97–8
   force majeure   126–7
   frustration   127–8
   goods and services   99–101
   holding writ   185–6
   implied terms   110–14
   liability   75, 113, 120–25, 133, 147
   limitation of actions   131–2, 148, 182–5
   limitation of liability   110, 113, 120–25, 133, 134–5, 154
   losses   134

mitigation 13–6
multiple parties 185–6
'non-derogation from grant' 125–6
non-incorporation 80–81
novus actus interveniens 137–8
offer and acceptance 108–9
outsourcing 97–9
privity 80, 144, 150, 178
reasonableness 125
remoteness 135
software 83–4
    development licences 86–7
    licences 78–85, 87, 111–12, 181–2
    maintenance agreements 87–92
    sales 87
    warranties 84–5, 116–20, 136
solution providers 101–4, 138
specific performance 138–9
standard of proof 143
statute 114–15, 185–6
termination of contract 139
see also tort
contracts 10, 27–8, 43
    audit xii, 28, 76–7, 94
    due diligence 169
    existence of 108–10
    investigation 52
    leasing 95
    pre-contract 106–7
    sale of goods 95
    warranties 71–2
copyright 78, 87, 123
corporate manslaughter 161–2
corporate standards 72
costs 9, 61

damages *see* contract law
data 50–51
    export 177–8
    input forms 51
    protection 175–8
Data Protection Act (1984) 175–6,
    Transfer Prohibition Notice 177
databases 84, 170
dates 3–7, 44–5, 47
    validation 6
decision making 35–9, 53–9
directors xiii, 10, 12–13
    disqualification 160
    duties 157–9
    negligence 160
    non-executive 156–7
    personal liability 155–62
    sanctions against 159–61
disaster recovery plans 30
dispute resolution
    alternative dispute resolution (ADR) 179, 180–81
    arbitration 179, 180, 189–90
due diligence 169–78
see also contract law

electronic mail 43
'embedded chip' systems 10, 28, 42, 43, 53, 66, 93, 96, 146
    investigation 51–2
    inventory 28
    reject 58–9
    repair 57
    replace 57–8
escrow 83, 85, 87
estoppel *see* contract law
evidence 186–9
    'balance of probabilities' 187
    expert 188–9
    record-keeping 187–8
European Union (EU) 177, 178
    Second Data Protection Directive 177

facilities management 97–8, 139, 171–2

Hampel Committee on Corporate Governance 155
hardware 10, 50
    audit xii

contract law 92–6
inventory 25, 27
investigation 43, 44–7
maintenance contracts 96
procurement 92–6
reject 58–9
repair 54–5
replace 57–8
health and safety 42, 57

IBM 4
implied terms *see* contract law
Institute of Electrical Engineers 51
insurance 161, 174
intellectual property rights 87, 92
Internet 45, 48, 51, 84, 145
inventory 10, 17, 23–31, 53, 61, 65
contingency plans 29, 30–31
contracts 27–8
embedded chips 28
format 24–5
hardware 25, 27
new equipment 66
software 27
systems 26, 49
investigation 43–52
consultancy 44, 62–3
hardware 44–7
software 46, 47–51
software tools 64–5
see also compliance
IT staff 56, 62
skills shortage 103

law *see* contract law, tort
legal audit *see* contract law
legal rights
statute 185–6
liaison group *see* project team
litigation 42, 154, 179, 179–90
'Calderbank letter' 189
holding writ 185–6
jurisdiction 181–2
limitation period 182–5
payment into court 189

summary judgement 188–9
see also dispute resolution
loans
interest calculation 5
losses *see* contract law, tort

mainframes 37
maintenance contracts 171
mergers
Year 2000 compliance 169–74
microcode 44–5
milestones 34, 71 *see also* planning
Millennium problem 3–7
extent 7
implications 9–13
raising awareness 10–13
scale xi, 11
timescale 101
Misrepresentation Act (1967) 151–2
multiple parties *see* contract law

National Computing Centre 83
negligence *see* tort
non-executive directors 156–7

'object code' 82
operating systems 7, 50, 56
investigation 47–8
outsourced IT systems 62, 97–9, 110

planning 33–9, 61–9
see also time line plan
prioritisation 41–3, 76
processing software 49, 50
project management 15–22, 33–9, 61
see also change management
project managers 15, 33, 164
project teams 16–17, 37, 71

Real Time Clock 46, 55
risk management xii, 42, 76

service providers 113–14
liability 122–4
shareholders 159, 160, 161

INDEX

software 10, 43, 114
  audit xii
  bespoke 50, 86, 100
  compliance questionnaire 195–9
  development agreements 86–7
  dispute resolution 180
  fit for purpose 111
  functionality 113
  inventory 27
  investigation 47–51
  legal nature 83–4, 115–16
  licences 78–85, 87, 111–12, 181–2
  platform 113
  reject 58–9
  repair 55–7
  replace 57–8
  sales 87
  shrink-wrapped 116
  warranties 119, 136
solution provider agreements 101–4, 172
  data protection 176, 178
  exclusion/limitation of liability 104
  warranties 102–3
source code 55, 56, 65, 82–3, 85, 87
staff 38–9, 59, 72 *see also* IT staff
Stock Exchange 159
suppliers 10, 171
  agreements 99–101
  compliance statement 100, 201–3
  duty 145–8
  hardware 45
  liability 122–4, 190
  negligence 105
  solvency 107
  statement of compliance 100, 201–3
  warranty 201–3, 205–6
supply chain
  liability 150–51, 179, 185
  management 99–101

take-overs
  Year 2000 compliance 169–74

Taskforce 2000 94
testing 53, 67–9
see also compliance, investigation
time line plan 34–5, 36, 39, 66
tort 89, 105, 132, 141–54, 160,
  causation 149–50
  consideration 146
  contrast with contract 141–2, 144–5, 148, 154
  contributory negligence 153
  damages 141–3
  defences 152–4
  duty 145–8
  foreseeability 149
  liability 147–8
  limitation periods 142, 143–4, 183–4
  losses 149–50
  mitigation 153–4
  novus actus interveniens 152
  remoteness 149–50
  standard of proof 143
  statute 185–6
'triage' xii

Unfair Contract Terms Act (1977) 122, 123, 151, 154
upgrading 48, 57–8
United States
  data protection 178

warranties 111, 136, 191–4
  express 71, 84–5
  implied 71, 84–5, 94, 110, 116–20, 148
  model 205–6
'windowing' 50, 53
Woolf Report
  Access to Justice 180
World Wide Web 51

'Year 2000 compliance'
  definition 85, 191–4
  warranty 95, 206
Year 2000-related losses 133–4